ORDINARY
WONDER

ORDINARY WONDER

Zen Life and Practice

CHARLOTTE JOKO BECK

Edited by Brenda Beck Hess

SHAMBHALA

Shambhala Publications, Inc.
2129 13th Street
Boulder, Colorado 80302
www.shambhala.com

9 8 7 6 5 4 3 2

Printed in the United States of America

♾ This edition is printed on acid-free paper that meets the
American National Standards Institute Z39.48 Standard.
♻ Shambhala Publications makes every effort to print on recycled paper.
For more information please visit www.shambhala.com.
Shambhala Publications is distributed worldwide by
Penguin Random House, Inc., and its subsidiaries.

Library of Congress Cataloging-in-Publication Data
Names: Beck, Charlotte Joko, author. | Hess, Brenda Beck, editor.
Title: Ordinary wonder: Zen life and practice /
Charlotte Joko Beck; edited by Brenda Beck Hess.
Description: First edition. | Boulder, Colorado: Shambhala, [2021]
Identifiers: LCCN 2020033945 | ISBN 9781611808773 (trade paperback)
Subjects: LCSH: Religious life—Zen Buddhism.
Classification: LCC BQ9286.2 .B445 2021 | DDC 294.3/444—dc23
LC record available at https://lccn.loc.gov/2020033945

CONTENTS

PART FIVE: CONFIDENCE

PART SIX: RELATIONSHIP

PART SEVEN: WONDER

FOREWORD

by Jan Chozen Bays

CHARLOTTE JOKO BECK was a unique person. Somehow, this middle-aged secretary became a daring innovator, a person who was always on the front lines when it came to trying new ways to be physically and mentally healthy. I was among the group of younger students at the Zen Center of Los Angeles who followed her lead.

She took the EST training with Werner Erhard, so dozens of people at the Zen Center took the EST training. She bought a small trampoline, and you could look up at the second-story window of her apartment at night and see her head appearing and disappearing as she bounced. Others began bouncing "to improve lymph flow." She began race-walking with weights on, so many people took to striding the streets. Much later in life, because she didn't want to be a burden on the center as she aged, she took up Pilates, with a professional machine and a personal trainer, at a time when no one had heard of Pilates. She was eighty. When I saw her during this time, I was amazed that she seemed to have reversed aging, walking with more grace and talking with more clarity than she had before. She taught into her nineties.

I met her when she was an administrator in the Chemistry Department at University of California, San Diego. I think she actually ran that department of quirky professors from her desk. She related that when her boss was out of the office, people would line up to talk with her. She later said, "I learned a lot about how to do therapy in those years." She was a single mother of four, divorced from an abusive, mentally ill professor who came close to killing her. Only the chance appearance of a neighbor saved her life. These experiences made her blessedly impervious to her students' whining about their life problems, and made her very clear about what really mattered.

Joko became interested in Zen while attending a debate between a Zen master and a Christian minister. She was so impressed by the complete aplomb and palpable presence of the Zen teacher, Maezumi Roshi (Maezumi Sensei, at the time), that she began studying with him. She was then in her late forties. A close personal friend had developed cancer. This woman had eight children and meditated in the little room with her washer and dryer, the only place she could get any quiet. Joko was inspired by her friend's devotion to practice—especially her ongoing commitment to caring for those around her, even during her last days. Joko felt that her friend's meditation practice was manifested in her refusal to take narcotics so her mind would remain clear, even in her very peaceful death. She sat with her friend as she made the transition from this life, becoming "pure radiance." Joko was deeply moved by this experience, walking along the beach for hours afterward, aware that she had lost all fear of death.

She joined a meditation group in San Diego. Over the years, as the group evolved, others in her life began to attend as well, including several scientists and graduate students from the university. She was a determined student and began doing annual *sesshin* (a rigorous sitting meditation retreat) with Yasutani Roshi and Soen Roshi. Her daughters went to these intensive Zen retreats with her to spend time—albeit in silence—with their mother. After Maezumi Roshi opened his own center, she began driving two hours north each Saturday to the Zen Center of Los Angeles for *dokusan* (private interview) with him, and then driving two hours back home. Eventually, she retired and moved to the Zen Center to practice full time.

One by one, we followed her north and created a lively Zen community, a strange hybrid of a hippie commune and a Zen monastery, filled with young people hell-bent on enlightenment. Once again, people lined up in the hallway outside her apartment, waiting to talk with her. She said that although she was unorthodox in her approach to practice, Maezumi Roshi made her a teacher because he saw how students were naturally attracted to her. Joko's relentless focus on practice was infectious, and many people who practiced with her in San Diego and Los Angeles eventually became Zen teachers with centers of their own.

Joko became ordained and soon received Dharma transmission, becoming a much-beloved teacher. After six years of living and training at the Zen Center, issues of misconduct by Maezumi

Roshi caused Joko to break her ties with him. She moved back to San Diego, where she founded the Ordinary Mind Zen School. Her way of teaching was direct, insightful, deceptively simple, and matter-of-fact, sometimes wry. You might wince when she pointed something out, but you knew she'd hit the bull's-eye—some cherished "core belief" that was causing you suffering.

Joko was the first person I heard giving practical instructions in what we now call "mindfulness"—currently all the rage. She told us, "When you wash the dishes, just wash the dishes. Feel the warmth of the water, the slipperiness of the soap, the plate in your hand." She could turn Zen rituals into everyday practices. In this book, she describes adapting the Zen practice of *kinhin* (slow walking between long periods of seated meditation) by telling an exhausted doctor to walk mindfully down a hallway each day, and his discovery of the refreshment this brought to his body and mind.

In a sesshin with Yasutani Roshi, Joko had a first opening into what she called "real life." She described it as "horrible." A friend remembers that afterward, when they took walks to talk about Zen, Joko would often stare intensely, point her finger and say, "This is not real." In another sesshin, she had an opening into the emptiness of all things. It made her furious. She went to dokusan, yelled that everything was empty, and threw a small lamp at the Roshi. She related, "Like a good Zen teacher, he ducked, said, 'Get used to it,' and rang his handbell to dismiss me."

Although Joko is often characterized as a psychologically oriented Zen teacher, she felt that therapy did not offer ultimate relief from suffering. "Therapy gives relief; sitting gives freedom," she would say. "If you practice long and hard enough, and uncover your core belief, you won't need therapy. Instead of being self-centered, you will become life-centered."

However, she remarked that if people were not ready to practice deeply, she would offer them a simple, practical therapeutic approach to their issues. One student shared that she had started law school and, with a husband and baby at home, had been overcome by inner doubt and criticism, convinced that she'd made a terrible mistake. Joko listened to her long discourse and then asked, "Did you get any grades yet?" "No." "Why don't you wait until you get your grades to worry?" Her tangle of thoughts and overwhelming anxiety were instantly dispelled.

Joko did not offer bliss, observing dryly that "Sesshin is controlled suffering" and that "The only thing worse than doing sesshin is not doing sesshin." She emphasized the slow, steady change that is possible with long years of practice. She cautioned that you would not become completely unstuck or turn into a saint, adding, "But, you know, there's a tremendous difference between being all the way stuck and being unstuck 50 percent. Even 50 percent unstuck is 50 percent free."

Joko was insatiably curious, and because of her background in science, she was always interested in new approaches that might help her students. One student remembered that Joko had a "bottomless bag of tricks, and would pull something out and use it on us. And she would just as easily discard it." Once, she gave essentially the same Dharma talk ten Saturdays in a row. Some people noticed; some didn't. She had bread and water served unexpectedly for formal Zen meals, and enjoyed the reactions that came her way later. A regular part of sesshin was "eye-gazing": sitting for half an hour, looking into the eyes of a different person each day, noticing what was happening now—bodily discomfort, averted gaze, the mind wandering off, emotions arising.

If students presented with a litany of complaints, she would ask, "What's your sentence?" They had to pare down their "mental entanglements" to one or two sentences, to help them see through the story they were telling themselves over and over. In this book, you will find one of her favorite quotes, "Rest on that icy couch." She explained this practice as resting bodily in the physical sensations, thoughts, and emotions. If you return to that icy couch, hour after hour, day after day, it becomes a gateway to freedom and contentment with whatever life brings forward.

Joko had high standards for herself. She was an excellent pianist, and we all enjoyed the music that poured out of her windows during breaks. As she aged, she gave up playing because her fingers would no longer play as she wished.

She was accessible to her students in an interesting way. She had telephone hours eight hours a week. If you called in when someone else was on the line with her, you just kept calling, hoping to connect in the brief interval between the last student hanging up and the next one dialing in. People called in from all over the world—and this was still when you paid for long-distance calls by the minute.

Although Joko eventually shed many Zen traditions, ex-changing her black Zen robes for a simple blouse and long skirt, she was completely faithful to the heart of Zen practice—the long hours of silent sitting. She felt that five days of sitting still, silent, and experiencing everything that was happening in body and mind, internally and externally, would gradually open a person's awareness of their core belief. This in turn would begin to untangle the tangle of thoughts and emotions that lay at the heart of the suffering of the person's "false, self-centered life," a life that she called the "consolation prize." She was clear that this process was not easy—was often painful—but led ultimately to complete transformation.

I encourage readers to listen to Joko's talks on YouTube—watch and listen for a few minutes or more, so that as you read and re-read her words in this book, you can hear the warmth and straightforward clarity of her voice. And for heaven's sake, practice what she recommends, what she spent forty years doing and teaching: sitting silent and still, for long periods of time, experiencing everything that is happening in what you call your body, your thoughts, and your emotions. If you persist, you will find, as Joko did, an ease and a simple happiness in all that life presents you.

INTRODUCTION
by Brenda Beck Hess

MY MOTHER ALWAYS wanted to write a third book, but just didn't have the energy to do so in her later years. After her death, I would often look at the boxes of tapes of her talks, get overwhelmed considering where to start, and leave the task. After pre-evacuation orders were given for the Doce fire in Prescott in 2013, one of the deadliest wildfires in American history, I knew that at the very least I had to start digitizing those tapes to ensure their safety. With the intent of also hoping to fulfill her desire to do another book, one day, not long after the fire, I picked a tape semi-randomly from the collection.

I placed it into the Nakamichi tape deck purchased for this purpose, and listened to the first words of the talk: "If I'm ever going to do another book . . ." Jackpot. The process of listening to and digitizing these tapes began.

On that first tape, which recorded a talk she had given in 1997, she spoke about what she called "the core belief." Curious about how she developed this critical aspect of her teaching, I felt compelled to backtrack about a year and a half from that talk.

In the early part of 1996, she was supposed to come to Prescott to visit, but came down with the flu for the first time in her life. She was pretty sick, and apparently had lots of time for practice and reflection. When she started teaching again, she shared that she was in the process of clarifying another level of practice, revolving around the core belief. In a talk midway through 1996, she outlined the birth of a child. Before birth, the world satisfies all that is needed in the womb. After birth, however, the infant's needs can never be totally met by others. Unable to conceive that there could be an issue with the parents on whom the infant is totally dependent, a seed is planted: the problem must be with the young baby. The baby feels there must be something wrong with itself, and this is the foundation of the core belief. The infant then develops a strategy to get what it wants. The baby will cry, please, or be defiant (among other options) in its efforts to get its needs satisfied. There are many strategies, but all are aimed toward the same goal: feeling safe and loved in the world. Since the infant feels its very survival is at stake, it earnestly adopts these strategies, finding a few key ones that seem to work.

For most of us, these strategies continue and reinforce themselves throughout our lives. They congeal around a few key themes, into what Joko called "the basic strategy"—even though for the most part, as we grow up, they no longer work. The core belief is always a negative belief we have about ourselves, an opinion so painful that we will do almost anything to avoid feeling our abject sense of unlovability and worthlessness. The basic strategies are our ardent but deluded responses: fixed reactions in a fluid world.

Although she saw the core belief as a natural, nearly inevitable formation in a young child's development, Joko focused her attention on the places where practice can help us intervene: the ways that, as adults, we perpetuate our core beliefs through our moment-to-moment decisions about how we relate to our lives.

She spoke repeatedly about how the thinking mind is useful in elucidating the core belief. But, this clarification, while very important, is only the first step. While somewhat useful, stopping here would leave a practice that exists in the realm of psychology.

The crux of practice with the core belief is to continue on from mere psychological understanding and do the work none of us want to do. We must rest and sit in the experiential pain that is the very difficult heart of our practice. This is resting in the present moment. This is Zen practice.

The paradox is that when one truly rests in this pain, the experience disappears, and there is no pain; there is no one to experience the pain. This is not something we can try to do. The paradox of practice is that as we use tremendous effort to stay with this pain the best we can, it slowly erodes, and moments can arise of no effort—of just pain, just joy.

These are the moments one might call "enlightened." But, my mother rarely talked about enlightenment because that is already who we are. We just don't see it because of the false construct we have carefully crafted to try and protect this vessel.

For her, the constant study and investigation she did was for the purpose of helping her students see the problem and learn to practice with it.

One of her central teachings was for people to label their thoughts. She found we all have our own repeating patterns of thoughts, and the patient, often redundant work of becoming aware of these patterns through labeling can help us see our core belief and the basic strategy that derives from it. Once we clarify this, then we slowly develop the skill to see when these patterns arise. She points out that whenever we are upset, we have a good clue that our patterns are in action.

A second major element of her teaching is that the continued work of studying and unraveling our core belief occurs in large part through resting in our often tightly held body sensations in order to unmask the rage and pain within. She emphasizes that we have to do this bodily, experiencing sensations thousands and thousands of times. The thoughts become like bubbles, neither clung to nor amplified with a subsequent train of other thoughts. The body sensations become just that: sensations that are experienced and gradually weaken. Then moments of the joy, regardless of what is going on, appear, unmasked.

Joko also clarifies in her talks that our core belief, our strategies, our thoughts, and our body sensations—all that we think are so concrete—are nothing more than the experience of the present moment. She teaches that our internal agony is nothing other than enlightenment itself. How could the experience of the present moment, no matter what that experience is, be other than enlightenment?

The tragedy is that we don't see this. Thus, we avoid the experience of this moment. And we suffer. Instead of being that which is now arising, we cover it with our strategies. Instead of manifesting the compassion we are, we manifest a life that revolves around trying to make ourselves feel comfortable and safe. Joko clarified in multiple talks about how to do extraordinarily simple and exceedingly difficult work.

We hunger for the peace of resting in this moment, whatever it is. But, it is the hardest thing to actually do. It takes work. What we want is to feel comfortable. The paradox is that we have to be the agony of our core belief over and over until it just wears out, and what remains is the joy and peace of the present moment, whatever it is. The life that manifests is one of compassion, appropriateness, and usefulness.

My mother's practice was impressively relentless. As was her commitment as a teacher: she endlessly searched for ways to help clarify what the task of practice actually is. She read widely from many different sources in this search, taking from Buddhism, Hinduism, Christianity, and many nonreligious, philosophical, psychological, and New Age sources.

She returned to two books, in particular, over and over again in her life. The first one was *The Supreme Doctrine* by the French psychotherapist Hubert Benoit. The second one was *I Am That* by the Indian Shaivism teacher Sri Nisargadatta Maharaj. I share this in case you are interested in reading them yourself.

I recall, as a child, her scouring bookstores for books that made sense to her, that would support her in her own search for truth. In later years, she looked for books that furthered her ability to help her students to understand what is entailed in practice, and by understanding it, be more able to do the work involved in practice.

When my mother was working on her first two books, she would fuss over each sentence, trying to make sure it clearly communicated her intent. At the same time, she would laugh and tell me that, in Zen, there is only ever one talk to give.

I never studied formally with my mother, but consider her to have been and to continue to be my teacher. What a gift it is to listen to her tapes, transcribe them, and help in the editing process. She remains alive, and I gratefully continue to learn from her words.

In the last year of her life, when her ability to teach with the finesse of her prior years was waning, another kind of explicitly clear teaching appeared. At first, I thought it was because her ability to expound on the teachings was gone. Then, I realized that her teachings were exquisitely distilled into one sentence: "You're fine." She would gently pat me on the arm and say, "You're fine."

I would like to thank Rachel Neumann for her editing. She took a year's worth of talks and made them cohesive and even more useful. I would like to thank Matt Zepelin at Shambhala for what I like to call his "smoothing" of the manuscript.

I am forever grateful to my mom. Her teachings saved my life. Her example of intelligent and diligent lifelong practice was the model for many of our own lives of Zen practice. She was willing to do that work. I hope you find her words useful in supporting you in returning to your life, the peace and joy that it is.

PART ONE

EXPERIENCE

The Only Thing We Need to Know

THERE IS ONLY one thing we need to know. It's utterly simple.

Our job, as humans who want to experience life fully, is to pay attention when we experience something.

To do this, all we have to do is to begin to be who and what we really are. That's it. We just have to be who we are, apart from all our ideas and our systems of dealing with life. That sounds delightful! Right? No way. Being who we really are means when we feel upset about a situation—when we are hurt or angry—we have to feel it. For some of us, these strong emotions make our body into a tight, miserable knot. Others of us get nauseous. Who wants to be that?

At first, we don't want to be in touch with the feelings because a lot of them, whether they are hurt, anger, or resentment, are born out of pain. And that pain feels, at first, like the last thing we would ever want to meet.

But when we truly experience what we are, whatever it is at every moment, there is freedom. Sometimes, people say to me, "Oh, yes, I'm in touch with who I am. I know my body is tight." That's not experiencing. For one thing, when we say "I" know "my body" is tight, we're already separating us, our knowing, and our bodies. We are assuming there is an "I" knowing "something else." The world is split. When the world is split, there's no peace. There's no freedom.

We might say, "But I know I'm suffering. I really feel it." That's not experiencing. When you are truly experiencing, you are not feeling the suffering or the anger; you *are* it. And I say: be what you are.

The word "experiencing" confuses some people. Experiencing doesn't mean something fancy. It doesn't mean anything more than, just for a second, being without the thought. It is whatever you are when you're not thinking about yourself. Just let your mind be quiet for two seconds. You feel whatever you feel; that's it.

Now, if you're really upset, naturally the body will be contracted in a more interesting way, you might say. But, most experiencing doesn't feel like anything much. Yet, when you can sit, say an hour or two, just experiencing, your life transforms at a tremendous rate. It's nothing spectacular. It doesn't mean thoughts won't come up, but it's like the thoughts bubble up out of the water, you experience them, and they disappear. What we usually do is follow these thoughts in our head, creating a fantasy, instead of letting the thoughts just bubble up and disappear as they naturally do.

Now, you can't *try* to do any of that. You can't try to let go. That's silly. Who is letting go? You can't try to fix yourself; you can't try to be an accepting person. What you can do is experience not accepting something. How many minutes can I just sit and be that? Most people can do it for about three or four seconds. The more we experience, the less we need things to be different. The less attached we are to judgment. And, needless to say, a life that grows from that kind of practice is more compassionate, more open, and more peaceful. It doesn't mean you don't fight for things or you don't act. But, you do so from a place of quiet and attention.

Going into real experiencing can feel like a tremendous loss. And it is a loss. It's a loss of who we believe we are. We lose what we think of as our identity. That's frightening. Of course, we don't really lose anything. But what we're afraid of is that we have to give up all our ideas about "I'm this; I'm that. I have to have this; I have to have that. He doesn't love me; it's a terrible life." In experiencing, there is none of that.

You can say, "But, I don't like a lot of those thoughts." You may not like them, but they are familiar. We'd rather be with the familiar than to keep diving into the unknown. That's why practice is hard—but it is possible.

The Secret to Transformation

We have a life that's happening all the time. A wonderful, fluid, amazing life, which we may like or dislike. But there it is, all the time. And we have a very fixed, narrow, little set of behaviors with which we try to process this vast experience.

The secret to experiencing the whole of life is just to be whatever we are experiencing. Say we manage for a few minutes to feel whatever we feel as opposed to running from it, thinking about it, analyzing it, taking a pill, getting drunk, or whatever we do so we don't have to feel it. If we can truly rest with it, be friendly and curious with that pain, we can begin to transform. When we live with a thought on top of everything, the pain is held tight. It can't move. It can't do a thing. It just sits there and drives you crazy.

When we can let go of the thought-based, personal desire for things to work out a particular way, for the first time, the pain that we feel can begin to open up. And when it opens up, the feeling gets clear and quiet. And at the end, there's silence and wonder. Finally, there's nothing—just wonder. Underneath all of our difficulties, there's this well of silence, which is real wisdom. Whatever you want to call it, it's there.

What Do You Really Want?

WHAT IS THIS life, and what is our part in it? For most of us, on most days, life consists of very ordinary tasks. Do I need to go to the grocery store? Should I call that person? What do I have to cook, clean, care for, or do? This is often what life consists of, and it can be wonderful. But if we don't, at some point, pause to sit and investigate, life can develop a flavorless quality. It's like eating sawdust. In the daily busyness, we forget something. That something else is at the core of our practice.

To return to the flavor of our lives, to get curious about what it actually feels like, we need to clear a little space. Maybe we can only clear two minutes. But those two minutes—if we truly take the time to stop, get curious, and fully experience them—can be a strong beginning.

Our human desire is that we want life to go our way. We don't want to be too cold; we don't want to be too hot. We don't want to be too hungry. We don't want to be uncomfortable in any way. It's fine to try and make ourselves more satisfied and more comfortable, but when the whole objective of our life is to be more pleased, more comforted, or more anything-like-that, then we've lost our way.

Much of our meditation practice is spent looking at the personal messiness that we live in. In sitting with the messiness, we can get to know it and learn to be comfortable with it. It's not that we get something tangible; we just get to more fully experience our life as it is. We become more available to life as it happens.

I used to sing in The Messiah, a Christian chorus. We sang a song that went, "His yoke is easy and his burdens are light." There are the burdens of life. But, as we stay with practice, we feel different about our life after a while. The yoke is easier and the burden lighter. Does that mean that sitting is easy? Not at all. Anybody who sits knows that it's never one thing. We enjoy it. Or we hate it. It's boring. We get restless. We don't want to be here. But the ability to stay with life as it is, which is all that is necessary, increases. Slowly, slowly, slowly. The practice is never-ending.

A Peace That Passes All Understanding

In the Bible, there is a line in Philippians 4:7 about a peace that passes all understanding. Isn't that what we all want? I don't think that kind of peace is some unbroken bliss. That peace is all the ordinary hardships and difficulties and stupid things that we all live through. When your understanding increases, the peace is right there in being too tired, in being treated unfairly, in being confused, and even in being sick of the whole thing. Peace and these experiences are not two different things.

What do you really want? Do you just want to be comfortable? Maybe, in this moment, the answer is yes. Perhaps you've had such a hard time lately that you want to relax and enjoy yourself.

It's okay to enjoy yourself, but having the conviction that comfort is all you need to attend to is the error. When comfort or pleasure is the only focus of our life, then we miss out on life itself. It's easy to miss it. We think, "Well, maybe next year." Maybe we have next year, but maybe we don't. Maybe we only have ten more minutes; we don't know. Sometimes, our time comes to an end very, very early. We don't have forever. Life is always short. It goes by in a twinkling of an eye. You can't do this work next year. You have to do it now.

Just Snow, Just Now

There is neither heaven nor earth,
only snow falling constantly.
—*Kajiwara Hashin*

THIS IS AN old Japanese haiku from 1864. It is the only poem of Hashin's that has survived. You may think, "Isn't that nice; the snow is always falling." But, let's change that a little bit. Suppose I'm sick, and this poem went, "There is neither heaven nor earth, only illness pounding steadily." Or, "There is neither heaven nor earth, only old age approaching steadily."

Sometimes people come into the Zen Center and ask me if I know the meaning of life.

Well, of course, I do: only snow falling constantly. There is only illness, only separation, only clouds. Happening and happening and happening. Life isn't miserable or terrible. It's just what it is, and that can take the form of severe misery at times, tremendous joy at other times, or some feeling between the two. "There is neither heaven nor earth, just poached eggs sitting on the table." Whatever it is, right here.

I sometimes see old friends who are, like me, approaching what we call old age. Some of them are watching the years go by with increasing bitterness. The bitterness, the resentment comes when we think life should be other than what it is for us. Each of us could describe our lives in such a way that they would seem miserable. See, there's a difference between being in the illness or in the snow and being miserable.

I was sick for many months over the winter. Do you think I liked it? No way! I didn't pretend to like it one bit, but I wasn't miserable. The "miserable" would come from the belief that I shouldn't be sick. How come I shouldn't be sick? If I'm sick, I'm sick. Of course, we do what we can to stay well. But, when life is what it is at this second, we have to abandon the never-ending judgments that we tend to make about everything. As soon as I was getting better, I made a judgment about my future: I thought "I'm never going to get sick again!" That was illusion popping into my head: "I'll do this and this and this and this, and I can control my health." You know what? It won't work. Sooner or later, I will get sick again.

In real old age, bitterness is obvious: it's in the mouth, the way the face is, the way the body is held. When you're young, the seeds of bitterness can hide as hope in something outside of yourself. Someone is going to take care of me, that wonderful person I just haven't found (yet). Or that perfect job, if someone would just see how good I am for it. Or, perhaps you think you will find the perfect practice that is going to make you enlightened if you just stick with it. Then you get disappointed or resentful when it doesn't appear or doesn't work. Of course, we can, and should, change things that don't work for us. But when we have an agenda that it must work for us, the disappointment and resentment arise, and therein lie the seeds of bitterness.

Do you think your meditation practice is going to make you happy? It's not. Is it going to change things? Probably in some ways, but maybe not in ways you like. Is it going to keep you from getting sick? It helps, over the years, because you don't rip yourself up quite as much. But I don't know of anyone who doesn't get sick. Does it keep you from getting old and eventually falling apart? No. I haven't met anyone yet who doesn't do that, eventually.

There is neither heaven nor earth, only _____. Only you know what you fill in here. People sometimes bring up the word "enlightenment." But enlightenment isn't something we march toward, and one day, somehow, we grab it. Enlightenment is the ending in yourself of that hope for something other than life being as it is.

Giving Up Hope

None of us want to give up hope. Being hopeful, and then losing hope, then gaining hope—this is another form of the snow falling.

There is a film called *Dead Man Walking* about a Catholic nun who's working with a man on death row. At the end of the film, someone says to her, "I wish I had your faith." And she says, "It's not faith really; it's work." I thought that was a very insightful line. What is the work? You could see her struggle with herself and her own reactions as her relationship developed with the person on death row. It wasn't easy for her. He was obnoxious and unkind. There was neither heaven nor earth—only, in the case of this man, nastiness and arrogance appearing constantly. The film showed the work she had done that had enabled her to care for him as he was. Some people are not easy. We don't want to care for people as they are. We want to care for them after they've made a few changes. You know, just a few. Then we might consider it.

The Catholic nun had to give up hope that the man on death row would be different than he was. If you hope, you're thinking. The reality of practice is just to be. Hope is really a thought that maybe it will be different someday.

The snow falling constantly is the great mystery. The person we live with is the great mystery. There's nothing that isn't the great mystery. And we say there is neither heaven nor earth because there is just this moment, whatever it is: snowing, raining, being sick, being well, being inspired, being bored. If you want your life to be what I think you know it already is, then doing the work is your only choice. It's not easy. There isn't some magic in Zen practice. It's not going to change you the way you expect. It will not give you anything you think you deserve. But when you do the work of being with exactly what is, slowly, unexpectedly, transformation happens.

Up, Down, and the Space In-Between

WE KNOW INSTINCTIVELY that for many plants, the winter cold, bareness, and withdrawal are absolutely essential to their later blossoming and growth. Most of us know this, but when it comes to our own lives, we don't always see it. We don't see the periods of confusion, misery, or mild depression as fruitful. We don't see that they're necessary for growth. We're much more likely to think there's something wrong with us and that we need to do something or take something to counter this down period.

The minute something's wrong, we run to the doctor and see if we can't get a quick fix. This is one of the reasons antibiotics are so overused that they're losing their effectiveness. Western culture tells us that if something does not please us, that if it feels disturbing or wrong to us, it should have an immediate antidote. I had a student from Nebraska tell me that she didn't know what was wrong with her meditation practice, but for the last two weeks, she'd felt sort of down. She really didn't feel bubbly, like she liked to feel.

So, what's wrong with her practice? Nothing. Absolutely

nothing. What's wrong with feeling down for a few weeks? I'm not talking about major depression here. As human beings, our emotions are constantly shifting, sometimes within a week, a day, an hour, or a moment. We may be going along fine, and then suddenly there's a dip. Our spirits rise and fall.

We may know intellectually that we can't have the light without the darkness and we can't have up without down. But, when it comes to our own thoughts and emotions, we want to live full-time in the light. We think there's something wrong with us or our meditation practice if we can't make everything feel just fine.

But this misconstrues the purpose of practice. Practice isn't about making things fine; it's about seeing that life is in alternation all the time: life and death; winter and summer; confusion and clarity. No matter who we are and what we do, we will experience these fluctuations, these highs and lows. There's nothing wrong with us. We don't practice meditation to make things all better. The purpose is not to get to the up. We think if we do it right, we can get to a happy positive place and stay there. Would that be a great place to be? Not necessarily.

We practice so we can be at peace at any point, no matter where we are in the up-and-down curve of our lives. With practice, we can see with more clarity and be present with what is, whatever it is, right at this second. This all sounds great in theory, but when the down-dip happens to us, we don't like it. That's fine. We don't have to like it.

What Is Joy?

What does it mean to practice in such a way that we become attuned to the up-and-down reality of life?

Sometimes, the downs are more frequent and deeper. We get laid off. We suddenly feel physically terrible and don't know what's wrong. Our partner leaves us or we leave them. Our children leave us or they return home. With age and illness, sometimes the dips come more often. But our learning accelerates because we begin to understand that life is swinging up and down all the time. It won't just stay still so we can feel good. It's that foolishness of wanting things to always stay the same, to stay good, that keeps our lives from being joyful.

To be joyful is to be at whatever point on that up-and-down swing that we are. We're always going to be somewhere. That doesn't mean we don't take care of things, like losing a job or being ill. We take care of what needs to be taken care of, but without the demand that it be taken care of right now, immediately, and forever. The thought that I should be joyful at the bottom of the trough is a thought. It's a concept. The reality is that when we experience the moment fully, for whatever it is, joy is revealed. But we don't have to do anything for that reason; joy just is.

That joy is available at any point.

When we can be absolutely just where we are, there is a surprising and easy joy. This is a very basic thing for all of us. When we understand practice as being okay with what is, that leads to joy. Joy doesn't mean the same thing as happiness. In the

United States, we have so much wealth and so many material advantages that we tend to think happiness is our right. And we like our gadgets. We think we can gadget our way to happiness. For the first time in my life, I have a dishwasher. I always thought that, cooking for one person, I didn't need a dishwasher. There were just a few dishes. But *I love* that dishwasher. It's just wonderful. And I see that if I didn't have a dishwasher, I'd be all right. I'd adjust to that in a day or so. Happiness is the "up-up-up." Joy is the peace in what is. It shouldn't be any way other than that.

Joy is what's going on, minus our opinion about it. It means that life and me, we're the same thing. It's just "That's what's going on." That's joyous.

You might already know this. But when you really know it in your body, you feel it. You know joy in what is. You don't get thrown so much by every little quirk in the way your life goes.

Noticing and Being

EVERYBODY IS STRUGGLING with something: their work, their marriage, their kids, the world around them. Even if they look outwardly successful, there is a constant flow from one crisis to another. Even those few who are not struggling often feel a sense of longing or a sense of conflicts that are bubbling just below the surface. We may not have what we call outwardly big problems, but there's always something. If you leave a human being alone for a little while, struggles come up.

What causes our struggling? If we come to a sitting meditation practice thinking that if we wear a certain thing or sit in a particular way and believe we'll find an answer to this question, we'll be disappointed.

It's easy to get caught in the trappings of practice. There are a lot of things about practice that can be very nice, but they're not crucial. It's fine to wear robes, but it's not crucial. It's fine to chant, but it's not crucial. It's nice to have a very simple beautiful space to practice in, but it's not crucial.

We come to a sitting practice not to get answers but to become more aware. Sitting is simply to maintain awareness. It's not something fancy. To maintain awareness is to be alive as a human being. There isn't something special called Zen practice. We just try to maintain awareness, as much as we can. By awareness, I mean awareness of our mental activities, awareness of anything in our own body that we can notice, and awareness of the environment in terms of the air temperature, cars, the heat, anything that you can pick up outside yourself. Awareness; awareness; awareness.

Awareness and Labeling

Becoming aware of your own mind is the first skill of sitting practice. When you first begin to pay attention, it can be a real shock to see what goes on up there. There is judgment, bitterness, and a lot of other stuff. To really see the activities of the mind is the first step: to label those thoughts.

This can feel dull or pointless at first. Who wants to do that every day? Thought: "I could think of something better to do." Thought: "It's kind of fun after all." We're changeable, see? Ten minutes ago, I didn't want to talk. Now, it's fun. Our thoughts are not to be relied on. They just come and go. Are they important? No, they're not important. But until we know our thoughts a little bit, we believe them. "Oh, I'm a worthless person. Nobody loves me." It's a thought. We believe stuff like that. "I can't do anything right." Or, "I'm better than other people. Maybe they don't see it, but I know."

When you label your thoughts, be like a court reporter. You're just taking it down. I doubt if a court reporter even knows what they're taking down. They just automatically take it down. They're not judging or analyzing; they're just recording. As soon as we're aware of a thought, we tend to analyze it: "Now, why do I have that thought?" "Why does this come up?" "How does that relate to that?" That's not awareness. Awareness is just really seeing what happens.

You don't have to label thoughts the whole time that you're sitting. Just try it for two to three minutes. The thinking we do is remarkably repetitive. So, you don't need to label for the whole time you sit.

After a few minutes, see if you can pause the labeling and experience a little bit. Don't worry—the sort of things we're spinning with are certain to be back. You know you're not missing a thing. They're not some precious prize. You can very well say to them, "Enough of you for now. Let's see what else is going on here."

Become aware of the complete sensory scene that you can enter when you aren't thinking. Experience the body and listen to the sounds around you. You might be able to pause for ten seconds or ten minutes. That's a really long time. Then the obsessive thinking shows up again. Because the minute you go back to awareness, since we don't like that very much, the mind will, in a very short time, begin to think.

Then you start to label again. It sounds dull. In a way, it *is* dull. But it's only dull if you're not interested in your life. If you find it dull, just know: you're not interested in your life but in the mental version that you cook up about it.

As we keep noticing, we get to know ourselves in a different way. We become aware of our minds. We cool down. We begin to watch this sea of stuff that runs through our minds. It's not good or bad; it's just stuff. The more we watch it, it assumes a different place in our life. Over enough time, it calms down somewhat. On any given day, you still might get attached to a thought. We still struggle. But when we notice that thought, if we're really honest about what we're thinking, we then begin to have other kinds of thoughts. "I'm a terrible person for thinking that. Oh, I shouldn't have a thought like that." We often miss this second layer of thoughts. We have to label everything—everything.

The honesty we develop about ourselves when we watch our minds is crucial. This is the first important step: get to know our own mind, become aware of our own tendency to latch onto our thoughts.

Experiencing Our Lives

When we take a moment to become aware of what is *underneath* our thoughts, we begin to understand not just our minds but also our experiences. This is the crucial second step of practice. This step is the only thing that works if we want to transform a life that goes chaotically from one struggle to another. We have to turn away from that sea of thoughts that we're playing with and begin to really feel what's underneath it. We have to *be* it.

When you begin to live life from this place of honestly experiencing, even when the experiencing is painful, a revolution takes place. It will eat away everything that you thought you were. Very, very slowly we move away from our self-centered view of things. Suppose I have a real stew in my life and I get stuck thinking the same thing over and over again: "I hate it. I can't stand it. I think it's unfair." It's a whole mishmash. And I'm going over all of it: what they said, what I said, what's going to happen next. This is what the average work-environment is like. Everyone is smiling sweetly, of course. But underneath, there is a stew of thoughts and emotions. Human situations, when you get four or five people together who don't practice, tend to be lethal. It's very easy to get caught in the swirl of judgments of yourself and other people. Often, we get caught in our thoughts and we act from this place of anger and judgment, and then our actions produce more anger and judgment.

It can take a lot of time, a lot of practice, to even know what we are experiencing, because we will use everything—all our conscious and unconscious defenses—not to experience what we're experiencing. Resistance is a major part of practice: "I don't want to sit today. It's too hard. I'll sit every day next month. I want to find a practice that makes me feel good."

I want to feel good too. But *really* feel good. Not dressing things up with something that's tinsel. And the thing is, we get around to feeling things one way or another. So, slowly we learn to go toward experience with less resistance. Because it's the only thing we can do.

This ability to experience is what makes for an exciting human life, one that's opening up. Fresh. The trees look different. People look different. As you embrace the suffering of life, the wonder shows up at the same time. They go together.

Practice Is Just Life

These are the two crucial elements of practice: to watch our mind and notice our thoughts, and to fully experience what is underneath them. But these practice elements only matter as much as our ability to apply them in our lives. We tend to think of practice as some strange thing instead of seeing that it's just our life, that it cuts through all the illusions we like to *think* are our life.

What we are learning we are only learning if we can bring it to all the events of our life. Everything is our practice. From the way we talk to people at work to the way we treat the people we see every day. This is crucial.

I notice in my own practice the one thing that slowly, slowly, slowly diminishes is any desire to fix anyone else. As far as I'm concerned, more and more, they're just fine being the way they are. I don't mean that I say they're fine while actually thinking they should be more how I think they should be. When I say they are good just the way they are, there's no rippling inside.

When you really and truly think someone else is okay, do you know what happens to them? Without anybody analyzing or thinking it, they feel, "Oh, at last, there is someone who thinks I'm okay just the way I am." This transforms a person. This is what we're all waiting for. You're not waiting for words of wisdom about how you should be. What most of us are waiting for is someone else to really think you're okay with all your warts, just the way you are.

Life as It Is

You don't have to like or accept people as they are. You don't have to accept anybody. "Accept" is a judgment, something you think you should do. But we do get to have more awareness of how we experience other people. The less we try to control this person or this moment, the more we can experience our own lives.

There's no way to get life exactly the way we want it, because it's changing so rapidly. What's okay this week will be blown to bits the next week. Life doesn't work. It can't work. There's nothing called "life." There are just enormous energy fields changing at tremendous speeds. You can't even hope that it will work; you can only enjoy it.

Life is always just the way it is. I might hope at my age that everything just ticks along perfectly. All that practice! But the fact is, it ticks the way it ticks.

PART TWO

THE CORE BELIEF

That Icy Couch

At least let me rest on that icy couch.

—*Hubert Benoit*, The Supreme Doctrine*

WHEN WE PRACTICE, we begin to understand our mind. And we begin, underneath our thoughts, to experience for the first time. Once we see underneath all the thoughts we have covering up our experience, what does that feel like? That unknown place is where the practice is, not in the endless analysis of our thoughts.

And when we experience without reacting or judging, we can start to get curious about what we're experiencing. What is our core self?

Our first work is to know ourselves. This is a lifelong task. Because to know ourselves requires returning to and uncovering

---

* Editor's note: Hubert Benoit (1904–1992) was a French psychotherapist and writer. My mom first read Benoit's *The Supreme Doctrine* in the mid-1960s. She felt it was an extremely difficult read. She returned to it over and over throughout her life, and I still have her original dog-eared copy. The sentence from that book used as an epigraph here, and which she paraphrases in this talk, stuck with her most of all. This was probably the most important, influential book she ever read for her Zen practice.

beliefs and decisions we made when we first formed our identity, many years ago.

The Birth of Our Core Belief

Before we are born, we actually have it pretty good. For most of us, everything suits us in the womb. We're warm enough. We have enough to eat. Nothing threatens us. The minute we are born though, we no longer experience that totality of being fed all the time in a warm, peaceful environment.

It doesn't mean that our parents are not good parents. There's no parent who can supply the craving of an infant for total love and safety. The infant's view is that they should have everything they want immediately. It's just not possible. We aren't physically equipped to serve anything, even a baby, in that way. So, very early on, the infant, without thinking, of course, begins to get the idea that this is a rocky road out here. Perhaps there's even a preverbal version of the thought, "I'd really like to go back, but here I am."

The baby doesn't know what to do, so as it grows into a child, it works out its own plan. And when things go wrong for you as a young child, as they will, you can't conceive that it's because the adults around you might be something less than perfect. You can only conceive that there's something wrong with you and that is why you're not getting this thing you need. The only answer is that there's something individually wrong. That "something wrong" calcifies into something negative, which I call the *core belief*.

The reason you're not getting what you need as a small child has nothing to do with you and everything to do with the grown-ups and the world they live in. But from the standpoint of this developing little human being, the belief arises that there's something wrong with them: "I'm unworthy." "Good things can't happen to me." Depending on the exact circumstances you went through as a child, your belief will have its own tenor. No two are precisely alike, but they're always some form of "There is something wrong with me."

It is excruciatingly painful to have this belief running your life. Babies can't stand it any better than anyone else. Since they're so smart—and they're very smart—they quickly begin to devise ways of handling that. And, if the total love just doesn't seem to be appearing naturally, we begin looking for it somewhere else and devising means of getting it. Depending on what you learned and were taught, this may look like anything from "being good" to "acting out," from trying to disappear to making a big fuss.

The Nature of the Core Belief

Every single person over the age of two or three has a core belief—it's just the nature of being human to have one. This core belief is not something true. It is always negative. This is because it is a product of the ego or separate self, the nature of which is to feel threatened. Nothing is truly separate, and so if we feel separate, we feel threatened. This separate self views life as something that either might please me—but I can't count on this—or threaten me. So, there's always tension and uncertainty there.

As small children, when we feel threat or actual pain, we try to separate from it. Usually, without conscious thought, we have to figure out how to handle this very difficult and even potentially life-threatening situation that, without any fault of our own, we find ourselves in. It is in figuring out how to respond to something out of our control that we formulate a negative belief about ourselves. This young ego, this "separate self," is frightened and angry, and the core belief arises out of this situation. We often first experience this belief as a scream: "*I can't! I won't! Help!*"

The older we are, the more this core belief gets hardened and buried, requiring more practice to uncover. Once we are old enough to have awareness of these structures, then I think it is appropriate to refer to the core belief also as a *core decision*—the decision to continue to live our lives in this anxious way.

The Hub of the Wheel

We all have a core belief. You may not know it yet, if you haven't thought about your life this way, but it's there. I'm not saying it's all you are, but it's there to some degree or another. If you've practiced for many years and are aware of it, maybe it's very weak and almost nonfunctional. But, it's there. And, it will come up, particularly in times of crisis. Our work is to know and experience the core belief so we can understand the way we sabotage ourselves.

Our core belief, for most of us, comes down to some version of "I feel worthless." That can look like: "I'm not enough." "I'm hopeless." "I can't do anything." "I'm disgusting." "I'm not loveable." There are a lot of variations, but always on the same separate, miserable state.

This belief is like the hub of a wheel. Out of it come the spokes, the systems, and strategies we use so we don't have to feel the pain of this false core belief—more on this below. But in short, it's too painful to bear. We can't stand to feel it. There's no one who can stand to feel absolutely unlovable. People who feel their core belief strongly and remain unconscious of it often withdraw more and more, and begin to do harm. I'm not just talking about extreme cases here—to some degree, we all do this. We cannot bear to feel so bad, so we develop our different strategies. Sometimes they're aggressive; sometimes they're placating, very nice, and charming. They can be anything. They may look wonderful in the eyes of the world, or they may look disgraceful in the eyes of the world, depending on how you're working this out within yourself. The important thing is not the particular content of your strategies but that you notice that they *are* strategies, and begin to trace the spokes back to the hub.

Finding Your Core Belief

You may not know what your core belief is. Most of us don't. We don't want to see it because it's always so bad. But, not seeing it is just self-protection. And it's not something you come to know through analysis or just playing around within your head.

A lot of people deny it. "I'm so comfortable with myself!" But, if you dig enough, if you meditate enough, there it is. When you really see it, it goes "*bing*," and you know that's it. It is always, always painful. It's like you're about to vomit. It's that awful feeling—that's the one. When you feel something, like a punch in the stomach, that "*umph*," then you know you've got it. And with that great awful feeling is the beginning of relief. Because it's not hidden anymore; you're beginning to relieve yourself of the tension of hiding this core belief.

Each time you felt threatened as a young child, each time you didn't feel safe, your mind let out a scream. Even if it was as simple as being three years old and seeing another kid take your favorite toy, and nobody tried to get it back from him. Even in such innocent situations, usually a scream comes out: "I must be worthless!" And for every one of these screams, the child makes a decision about itself. It's inevitable. Each one of these screams contributes to the mass of the core belief, the building feeling of who I think I am. Painful. Exceedingly painful. Each one of these is like a close-to-death feeling. And every one of us grows up screaming something. Maybe two or three things, maybe the whole caboodle. "Don't ignore me." "Just love me." There is one that is primary. Whatever it was, and is, for you.

Once the screams have solidified into the core belief, that pain has to be dealt with. It's too unbearable; you have to deal with it. So you begin to set up your requirements for life—your systems, your strategies—so you don't have to feel, at least in full-blown measure, the pain of that core.

Most of us spend years, decades, or our whole life, busy with these efforts to avoid feeling what's there. But practice offers another approach. When we sit day by day by day, we begin to develop—very slowly, very tentatively—the ability to return to the only thing that will give us peace, which is to enter right down into the pain of the core belief. You have to dive right into it and learn to live there.

It doesn't mean it looks any different to your friends; they won't see what's happening. But this is your practice, to learn to just rest in the pain. As Benoit says, "At least let me rest on that icy couch." There's nothing else to be done except to rest directly in this pain. When you're resting in the pain itself, you begin not to need the covers. You don't need covers for something that is already uncovered. You're in the middle of it.

At first, you just do it a little bit. Don't worry. We're not going to do it all at once. But, we have to be willing to do something. Sitting builds the power and the sensitivity so that we can be with ourselves. At first, we can do it for maybe ten seconds. Then, over time, three minutes, ten minutes. Finally, we can sit in dignity in the middle of that. Just sit there and let the pain and the misery be. That's the dignity of sitting.

When unreality (the core) meets reality, which is experiencing, then slowly the unreality just fades away. And you go back into your Buddha nature: your open, compassionate, loving self. You begin to recognize what's underneath the surface, what's underneath even that core belief. There you are.

See What You Do

We shall not cease from exploration
And the end of all our exploring
Will be to arrive where we started
And know the place for the first time.

—*T. S. Eliot, "Little Gidding,"* The Four Quartets

YOUR CORE BELIEF, this foundational perception of who you think you are, informs your way of dealing with your life. It's what I call your *basic strategy*. Your basic strategy is how you behave in reaction to the thought, "I am this; therefore, this is the action I must take."

I once knew a little boy who had a difficult and punishing father. This father was very strict. He yelled a lot and, occasionally, he hit his son. Now, naturally, this little kid had to do something to survive. He tried yelling back. That didn't work at all; he got physically punished if he did that. He tried ignoring his father. That didn't work. He tried agreeing. That didn't always work. Eventually, he found that the survival strategy that worked best was to be very quiet and docile. He became a sweet little boy who was almost invisible. That didn't work perfectly, but for whatever reason, it worked best, and he was able to occasionally get a little peace.

After a while, the boy began to unconsciously respond to everything in his life with this same strategy. If something happened that he didn't like, he would shrink from it and try to disappear. The strategy became automated, and as he grew into a young man, he used it in just about every situation. It might have been a very poor strategy for some situations and a great strategy for others, but it didn't matter; it was his habit now. And more than that, it was his basic strategy. He no longer had any choice. Whatever difficulties entered his life, he stepped back and tried to become invisible.

Eventually, he became an adult with only one way of dealing with difficult situations. But, as we know from experience, life is unpredictable. It's flowing, and it throws up all sorts of things. So, a simple, rigid reaction doesn't work very well. It doesn't feel good either. And yet, most of us have some kind of habitual, automatic reaction left over from childhood that we use for almost any challenging situation. This unconscious basic strategy might work pretty well for a while, but eventually it stops working.

Our strategies are all the ways that we do our life, particularly when we're troubled, so that we don't have to feel the pain of that core belief. We do all sorts of things, and they may look very different from one person to another. One person has to be busy all the time or talking all the time. Another person is always so quiet that you wouldn't know they're there. Some people will tell you off in a minute. Some people will never say anything that would hurt your feelings. Strategies. Strategies. Strategies. Unless you learn to know and explore your own strategy, it's automatic. It just runs. Once we have our set way that we handle life, that's what we do. And we'll do it until we're ninety-five. The thing that brings people to practice is when they begin to see that the strategy doesn't work.

For example, perhaps your core belief is "I can't." This is the belief underneath what you do. How people would phrase this core belief can vary: "It's impossible." "I just can't." "I'm worthless." "I can't do it." The strategy is how you deal with that belief. You develop whatever you think works with that. It might be complete withdrawal. If you're really hidden away, nobody can find you. That's one way.

Somebody like me would say I absolutely can't do it, so therefore I will do everything I can to do it well. It looks much better from the standpoint of the world, but it's not really any better. So, I was good at everything I did. I made sure of that because that was the only way I could handle the fear underneath. It looks good, but it's not a solution.

Now, if somebody told me I had to walk thirty miles today, I might say, "I can't do it." But, there's a difference between realistically knowing I can't do something and that core belief about myself that I can't do it, no matter what it is. They feel different, and you know the difference in your body between the two.

One of the hardest core beliefs is, "You can't make me do anything." It may not be stated that way, but it's there. If no one can make you do anything, you'll resist everything in your life. I think we all have a little of that in us: "You can't make me." There's held-over resistance to any kind of authority: "I don't care what you say. I may look like I mean it, but you can't make me. No way."

Becoming Aware of Your Basic Strategy

One way to see your basic strategy is just to watch and see what you do. The next time somebody does something you don't like, or you do something you don't like, what do you do? Because we're remarkably consistent, we will all do our strategy. Perhaps your strategy is quite active—performing, helping, accomplishing. A lot of success stories in our country are based on a core belief that says, "I'm nothing. I'm incapable. So, I'll spend my life proving I'm capable." That can be a very outwardly successful yet lifeless way to live. Or perhaps yours is more of a passive strategy—withdrawing, hiding, perhaps putting up a smoke-screen of excuses, even drug use.

The best way to become aware of what you do, of your strategy, is to notice an experience in which you really get everything you think you want, and then it still doesn't feel right. You're still not satisfied. Our basic strategy is always unsatisfactory. It's limited, and even if we don't feel actively miserable, we feel uneasy, unsatisfied. Once you get an inkling that no amount of stuff, no strategy, will actually satisfy you, then you begin to be interested in practice. Otherwise, you won't do the work. You'll just run toward your next strategy; that's all.

When we start to pay close attention, we begin to know all our strategies, which tend to just be variations on our one, basic strategy. When you are aware of your strategy, it begins to weaken. If you see that you think you have to talk all the time, for example, somewhere in the middle of your speeches, you'll go, "Oh, I'm doing that again." When you pay enough attention, it begins to enable you to return to the actual present moment, which of course can include your pain. It usually does. In some people, it's just numbness or something of that sort, but there it is.

There's nothing to judge about having a basic strategy. Once you see your strategy, what does it feel like? See if you can feel the experience underneath the strategy. The practice is in the feeling and knowing of the underlying experience, not in judging, critiquing, analyzing, or defending it.

The Wonder of Surrender

Sometimes we get right to the edge of the feeling underneath our strategy, and we veer off. This happened to me the other night at 2 a.m. Perhaps you know something about that. I could tell I was right at the precipice of awareness, and I wanted to swerve. Like anyone else, I didn't want to experience that which I didn't want to experience. It took a long time for me to be willing, finally, to just rest in this experience. Even after almost thirty years of practice, it's not easy. And when you finally see that you have no choice, it's a surrender. What are you surrendering to?

You can call it God or you can call it something else, but it is the present moment. We don't want to enter that present moment minus our ego, our preferred version of our self. If you truly experience your own pain without "I'm experiencing my pain"— without judgment or analysis, without even an "I"—you've given up your self at that point. Sometimes Zen teachers talk about how you die on the cushion. You give up your own personal version of life and just let it be. It's hard. But it's not impossible.

And then, the wonder happens. If there's wonder there, you may ask, "Why don't we just go there right away?" We don't go there because our whole life is predicated on maintaining this system that we're running. And this is true even though our basic strategy has never worked, never will work, and we even know that it doesn't work. But each time we hit a crisis, unless we practice, we come up with a new version of our strategy, a new excuse, a new way of analyzing it and getting control.

Practice is seeing what is there without our basic strategy. That's why it's okay to practice without altars or cushions. Personally, I think a little bit of formality is nice. It makes it special, in the same way you don't go to the prom in your shorts. But it's not the core of practice. Practice is returning again and again to this awareness, experience, and exploration. The fact that you had a moment of awareness three months ago doesn't have anything to do with anything. You have to get it now. Then there's that weightlessness almost. You know each moment as if it's happening "for the first time."

Our Central Work

ALL TECHNIQUES, ALL practices, and traditions—though useful, even extremely useful at times—are just approaches to the problem of our core belief and our impulsive, basic strategy for handling it. Our central work is to shift—very slowly, usually over a lifetime—from a self-centered view of things to a life-centered view of things. And I don't mean to shift from self-centered to other-centered—that's just an alternative strategy.

For a young child, the core belief can save their sanity or even their life. It has served us well. But it persists long past its usefulness. We grip it tightly because we feel, not knowing any better, that doing so will save us. If you have a core belief, for example, that you're no good, you'll grip on to that because it's rapidly covered by the thought, "I'm going to do everything so well that people will think I'm wonderful." The core belief and the basic strategy reinforce each other's necessity. We all are caught in that kind of maneuvering, trying to outsmart our core belief. That's all we've ever known. And, because that's all we've ever known, our core belief is very precious to us. It's scary to move out of that tight, rigid way of living.

But our core belief not only isn't appropriate as we grow up, it's also actually harming us. Being self-centered is poisonous both to ourselves and to those who have the good or bad fortune to meet us.

The shift from that self-centered, poisonous point of view to a life-centered point of view develops almost infinitesimally over a lifetime. It might not ever happen because our need to hold onto our self-centered point of view is so very strong. The nature of our self-centeredness means we really don't want to do any of this work; we just want to find a way out of the pain. That's okay. If you did nothing all your life except to label your thoughts and try to get back to your actual experience, you'd have a solid meditation practice. Because it's hard to maintain any practice. Our mind tells us that we're bored with it to cover up the fear of having to really experience the pain of our core belief.

True Self, No Self

We all have two ways of perceiving: we have our core-belief self and we have our true self. The core-belief self is saying, "Life has been so hard on me that I need to have these false assumptions about myself." Resentment, anger, and all sorts of emotions are tied up in that position.

Sometimes our behavior comes out of fancier core belief systems, compound core beliefs like, "You can't make me," "I can't do it anyway," and "I'm helpless." Our work isn't easy. Is there anyone who thinks it's easy? Not if you see what practice really is. I'm not trying to make it seem like doom and gloom. The doom and gloom come when you don't practice. That's the sad thing. Actually, the doom and gloom steadily subside over years of practice.

As I talk about the core-belief self and the true self, I don't mean that you have one self that's going to shift somewhere over to another self. It's all one self. But as your core belief gradually weakens, you will see differently, including seeing yourself differently. Our core belief causes us to see life as such a limited sphere, as if we have blinders on. We take this tiny sphere as the solidity of life, and we cling to it. The shift is to see that it's not solid, and that the sphere is just a minuscule part of a much larger whole. Our core belief has us seeing a tiny piece of something as everything, because our emotions say it is everything. With practice, our world opens to the wonder of experiencing that this thing we thought of as our self is just a tiny part of everything we see.

The Buddhist term for this experience is usually "no self." *No self* doesn't mean you evaporate. It simply means that your self, at any moment, is devoted to that which is appearing, the endless life that shows up second by second by second. No self is neither wonderful nor terrible. We're just here at this second. We create space and time, but life is just happening.

The true self, this no self, is incapable of judgment. It can't think about something as being good or bad. It's outside of space and time, and if there's no duration, there's no "unit" that can judge. No self is just moving, you might say.

People often come to Zen because they're looking for the true self. But you can't look for the true self. It's nothing; there's nothing to find. What you can do is to constantly work with the conditioned self, the one whose lens is the core belief. Because the conditioned self looks at everything through the distorted lens of the core belief, it can never see the world as it is.

We don't have to get rid of the core belief—that might be too hard—but we have to see through it. In this way, what is hard, thick, and fixed slowly becomes transparent, and we begin to see that it's just nothing at all. None of us can do this completely. One great Zen master says that we all keep a tiny bit of self-belief because it is what connects us to being human.

To truly feel when we're humiliated, hurt, taken advantage of, or whatever it is that's shaking our core—we don't really want to do that. I don't. But I can do it. I don't always get to it in two seconds; sometimes it takes a while. You can do it too. And you have a responsibility to do it, not because a teacher says so, but because your true self says so.

The Mind Is Not an Orphan

You need to understand precisely what your practice is about, and your mind is a wonderful tool for that. The mind is not an orphan. The well-used mind is a tremendous servant. Even still, in a given moment, we may or may not be able to do this practice—but we know this, and if we don't do the practice, we know what we're not doing. Sooner or later, as we keep—in one way or another—persisting, understanding falls into place, our core belief temporarily lessens, and we touch our true self, our no self. Maybe not all of it, but chunks of it. Perhaps we feel, for the first time, some satisfaction in our life. It's not some puzzling, worrisome mystery that we can't seem to get a handle on. Our lives are no longer utter confusion.

To reach a place of less confusion, even briefly, is an important step because these core beliefs are not trivial. They rip up your life. I'm not just talking about your Zen practice, whatever on earth that would be. They tear you apart. If, for example, your core belief is, "I never quite make it," as your life unfolds, you'll make sure you never quite make it. Instinctively, you know how to "not quite make it." After all, our core belief is familiar; we've had it our whole life. It's who we think we are, and until we sense another option, we don't want to budge from that. That's why practice is so difficult.

But with continuity of practice—really learning to employ the servant of the mind—we have more and more ability to see and experience life fully as it is, without needing or wanting it to be any different. This ability grows forever if you really practice. Also, since we are selfish, in the sense of wanting our lives to be joyous, practice unveils this joy. With this growing practice, we become less disruptive to our self and to others. In fact, our lives tend to become more cooperative, more creative, and more loving.

"I'm Sorry"

How do you know if you are practicing well? I find it to be the ability to be sorry, truly sorry, when you've hurt someone. This also includes being sorry when we hurt ourselves, although it's more obvious when we hurt someone else. Our self-centered self isn't sorry for anything, not really. It just wants to escape into a place that's not threatening or painful. So, it's really a hard task to stick with our practice, to begin to see how little we really want to say, "I'm sorry. I apologize."

No one is going to thank you for practicing. No one is going to put up a medal or a trophy for you. "You got to experience pain three times yesterday. Congratulations. You should get a trophy. Or at least a hug." But most of the work we do is in silence. You do it for you. And until you have some glimpse that you need to do it, that you hurt others if you don't do it, your work will be inconsistent. You hurt your partner, your child, your friends. That's why the growth of "I'm sorry" is an indication of some softening—softening in that core belief. "I'm really sorry I did that. I hate to admit it, but I'm sorry."

Continue without Thinking

The journey to a life-centered point of view continues without your thinking. Thinking won't serve it. But you can have an awareness of your core belief as you go about your practice. Whenever you're upset, you can be sure it's there. And as we just patiently plow along with our sitting practice, it also has a way of showing itself.

The more you practice, the more you'll notice when your core belief pops up. It's defending itself, but it loses power. "I can't do it. I won't do it. I'm incapable of doing it. I'll always fail." See how blind that is? It's never true. All that stuff is never, never true. Who you are is absolutely positive, benevolent, kind, and careful of how you live in the world so that you don't do any more harm than necessary. We all have constant slippages and failures. That's part of it. We're not talking about some perfection. We're human; we're not going to sprout wings, I don't think.

The more you practice, the more you'll be aware that the core belief pops up and then pops back down. It's not, as it perhaps once seemed, some powerful thing that constantly runs everything. It doesn't stay as long when it visits. And you see it even as it's happening. It gets kind of humorous after a while.

My core belief is "I can't do anything." That's ridiculous; I can do things. I know it's being ridiculous, so I just say, "Are you here again? Well, hi." And I go about my business. You don't have to believe that stuff. It's not the existence of the belief that's the problem. It's that we *believe* in its existence. The only way to pierce through the belief is by experientially staying with the pain that's at the base of that belief. That's our central work, and you can't do it by thinking your way through. It just doesn't work. That's why sitting is so important. It lets us experience sitting with everything that the core belief has been working so hard to keep us from feeling.

The Nature of the Self

There is a reality even prior to heaven and earth;
Indeed, it has no form, much less a name.
—*Zen Master Daiō Kokushi*

THERE IS A reality that has no form, much less a name. Beautiful and also true. We are nothing but the second-by-second manifestation of that reality. It's what we are, but we don't see it.

Most of us, whether through religion or rationality, try to grasp the nature of reality directly. We try to fit reality into a framework we can understand. But you can't screw a little screw into a big hole; nothing happens.

As I've described earlier, from the time we're very small, we begin to build up a belief about reality and about who we are. This is based on our experience of all that has happened to us— good, bad, or indifferent. The result of this belief might be called our individual personalities, our individual selves, our egos. Each one of us is different. Some of us might resemble each other more than others, but we're all different.

Once I have my core belief solidly in place and a sense of a "self"—a "pseudo-self" that is—built around it, then I can proceed as if I understand myself and my reality: I'm Joko, with all my little characteristics. There's nothing so wrong in it. In daily life, our conventional selves often serve us well. But if I really think that's who I am, inevitably a split takes place. I divide myself in two because I have to have one part of me constantly watching what I do, how I conduct myself, what I think. I also have to split myself off from the rest of the world so I can keep a good eye on it. It's not to be trusted, you know. We learn to be a little suspicious about everything out there.

Dr. Thomas Hora (founder of the discipline of metapsychiatry, integrating metaphysics, spirituality, and psychology) said, "All problems are psychological, and all solutions are spiritual." Because we believe so fully in the idea of the "self," we often think the problem of our unhappiness rests with ourselves. That's not all wrong. The amount of trauma you experienced as a child has a huge effect on you. And it's useful to do what you can to understand and heal from trauma. But we don't necessarily transform as human beings just from understanding what happened to us in the past.

Three Lists

If we want to truly transform our life—to transform our ability to understand and experience our life—then we have to know our self on all levels. To get a sense of how your self was created on the psychological level, I recommend everyone make three lists.

The first list begins with this sentence: "As a small child, I was trained to be . . ." Then, list everything that comes to mind. For example, I was trained to be "perfect," which meant never showing anger, succeeding at everything, getting straight As, and pleasing everybody. I was the quintessential good little girl. Everyone was trained to be one way or another.

The second list begins: "Right now, as an adult, I require myself to be . . ." How we were trained has a large effect on our ideas of how we should be now. So, for example, based on the training detailed in my first list, I might write down: "I require myself to be loyal, thoughtful, kind, patient, selfless, and calm."

In the second list, we notice how we've set up our life. One woman told me she's aware that she always sets up her life so other people will punish her. That's a deep, conditioned decision from way, way back somewhere. Once you've become aware of what you require yourself to be, you can watch yourself making decisions based on this idea as you march through your life. There are lots and lots of kinds of decisions you make, based on this idea of yourself. Here are a couple of styles these decisions can take: "If I avoid everything, that will help." "If I take charge and beat up the world when needed, that will work." "If I just manage to fail at everything, that'll work." There are thousands of such variations.

The third list gets very interesting: it's a list of the emotions hidden behind the second list. On my second list, I have: "I want to be loyal." Suppose I have a good friend who's sick in the hospital. It's Saturday afternoon, and I'm worn out. But still, I think I should go see her—not because I want to, but because my second-list requirement is that I'm loyal. And I will go see her, but beneath the appropriate action, there may likely be resentment. I'll go to see her partly because I love her, but partly because that's what "good" people do. Our third list helps us see the mechanism of the self that we've set up and believe in. This is the self we live out of: our core way of seeing things.

It's really important to see who we think we are. But what is the solution when you've seen it? You can see Mount Everest; Mount Everest just keeps sitting there. It doesn't do what I want it to do. It's the same way with all this knowledge we gather about ourselves. It will just sit there, waiting for us to notice and get curious, rather than react.

Quieting Our Reactivity

Our reactivity and judgment, and all the suffering they cause us, come from this idea of a separate self. I'm frightened for that separate self; I'm worried about it. I'm elated when things go well for it. I've set out all sorts of claims in its name. I think I have to have certain things for it. To some degree, we all think like this. But how much do we see through that, and in doing so, let it wither?

Creating a list of the feelings behind who we think we are helps us see what we feel when we act out of some rigid sense of self. It helps me experience the bodily tension of rigidly held emotion without the overlying thought of how I *should* be. I used to get incredibly angry, and act it out. When something would set off my anger, *boom!* It exploded. I wasn't always exploding, but the anger was there all the time. Slowly, I learned to notice when anger arose, before I acted on it.

Often, our problem isn't what other people do. Our problem is when someone violates our second-list requirement, showing what's underneath and exposing us to the unpleasant emotions of the third list. Again, this doesn't mean you don't respond. You still act. But when you really see your thoughts and experience your anger, you can act with more clarity and without as much anger, maybe none.

How does practice create transformation? I experience my anger now, without suppressing it or acting on it. Perhaps you experience your fear instead of running around it or rationalizing it. You stay with it and begin to do things that frighten you, not to be virtuous but so you are now able to directly feel the body sensation we call fear, and because doing the thing that frightens you is what needs to be done. It's very useful to do things you don't want to do—make that phone call you don't want to make, or whatever it is for you.

The Missing Step

With unfailing kindness, your life always presents what you need to learn. Whether you stay home, work in an office, or whatever, the next teacher is going to pop right up. I spoke recently with a student who doesn't like it when his wife tells him what to do. It isn't necessarily that he minds doing it, but he doesn't want his wife to tell him what to do.

We all have situations like this, and very few of us like being told what to do. Our first thought is usually, "I don't like it." Our second thought is often to want some solution. Then we have another "I" thought that discusses the first thought. Nothing gets solved; we just get increasingly tight, tense. What have we done? There's a step we've missed.

That missing step is to experience how we are feeling as we have that first thought. Get curious. Notice. We miss this step hundreds of times a day, and missing that step over and over is like never contacting the earth with our feet. When we think without truly experiencing, we're trying to live three feet off the ground. Our life lacks solidity and firmness.

Resistance and Persistence

If we don't do our sitting and our life with some attention, it's easy to lose the ground. It's easy to resist paying attention, to resist experiencing, because feeling things is a lot. It can be painful. For many of us, life itself can be increasingly painful. And sitting, actually experiencing things, slowly gives us space to feel and ease that pain. This gives us that motivation. Finding that missing step is a case of being patient and persistent.

We resist feeling that pain because experiencing it is not easy. But the act of seeing the resistance is part of the work we do, which allows us to have contact with our unwillingness. And the more contact we have with our unwillingness, the more the transformation to willingness begins to occur. It's just a matter of being persistent, of being willing to experience our unwillingness a greater and greater percentage of the time. We can't make ourselves willing. But, contact with our unwillingness gradually transforms it into willingness.

We get to know many things if we persist. Over time, people who are patient and who sit—for whatever reason they decide to sit—find that their resistance begins to break at some point.

We have to be diligent. Now, I don't mean that we sit and think about our practice all day. That would be silly. But we learn to watch for the signals, the daggers. The daggers are the thoughts of what we don't like, what's wrong with people, our hurt feelings, our judgments, and all the thoughts that keep us defending ourselves. Our personality, our ego, says, "Defend yourself against those daggers at all costs. Have lots of thoughts." The only step that counts, the one that puts you down back onto the earth, is feeling. After that first thought, just feel the pain of that dagger going in, really feel it; then something happens.

So, our life consists of the missing step. There isn't anyone here, including myself, who doesn't miss that step. I don't miss it as often, by any means, as I used to. The progress of practice is to notice, more quickly, when we miss a step. The tremendous knowledge we get from sitting with ourselves enables us to notice much more quickly when we miss a step.

And, through sitting, we develop the willingness to do that. Our belief in our thinking, in our separate self, gets weaker and weaker. You can see the difference in a person who sits regularly over a long period of time, and uses that time to notice and experience their lives. You can't even say exactly how they're different, but you notice it all the same.

Practice Is about Your Life

PRACTICE IS ABOUT what goes on with you in your life and how you feel as you live that life. What is important to you, what you struggle with, will change over time. But practice requires a continual return to exploring. As soon as we think we have figured it out, we've gotten stuck in an illusion.

Let's say you are eighteen, and the question of your boyfriend is paramount. There's something important to learn in that relationship. All relationships with other people start with a struggle to some degree: I want something, and they want something else. There's a clash, whether it's hidden or not. But, say you practice, you figure some things out, and the clash is resolved. You may have the feeling that you see more clearly now; you know what life is about. Perhaps a haze of happiness arises. But at some point, the very haze of happiness becomes just another boundary—you grow bored with this boyfriend and want a different one, or you sense that the relationship may be holding you back from other interests. The haze of happiness has turned into something you feel shut in by. There's something new to push against.

Perhaps you're in your thirties and you're in the wonderful business of dealing with children, which, as far as I'm concerned, will drive anybody crazy. As we deal with all that and learn to have some ease with it, perhaps, again, we have this feeling of, "Ah, I see what life's about. I know how to do this." And then the next challenge arises. As new areas of challenge begin to develop, we often meet each new challenge with resistance—this is the nature of life. We thought we had figured things out, and then there's a little bit of resentment that we still have more to learn and still have more pain to feel.

At each stage of our life, our practice is what it is. Almost imperceptibly, the things that we're interested in, and what we're working with, will begin to shift. Different questions arise: What is my life really about? Who is my partner? What is the meaning of my life? Or, as we age, what is death? In fact, the question of existence, of death, can arise at any time in our life. But when we're younger, it tends to get drowned out. Much of our lives is spent going after something we want: a job, a relationship, our kids to be all right, money, health. There are so many things to want.

Practice is what you're about. That's of major importance, to understand what you're working with in your life, and to begin to have some way of not making a mess of all that. But it's not all there is. At some point, the horizon gets wider. As far as I can tell, in a life of sitting, it never ceases to get wider and wider and wider. We're still occupied with the personal problems. Life is always about people, relationships, and whatever work we're doing. But if we truly begin to enjoy a regular practice, there are periods of resolution and a sense of something settling down within us that wasn't settled before. The base of life becomes stronger. There is still struggle, but our sense of solidity gets stronger and stronger the longer we practice. We get much more comfortable with this idea of just living.

A Substitute Life

Our practice is always to uncover what's blocking our awareness of the wonder that is life. The main way we obscure the wonder is by having a "substitute life." This is because the only possible response to a core belief, if it's not recognized, is to lie to yourself and everybody else. You may not call it that, but that's what it amounts to. To live through such a lie is not a genuine life but a substitute one. It goes through the motions and gives the appearance of our life, but is born out of the illusory world of the core belief.

I'm always amazed at the number of people who, underneath a successful or charming surface, feel that they're worthless. So many people feel like their only use in life, really, would be if somebody put them on the end of a mop and cleaned up things with them. They think that would be quite appropriate.

That's not true of everybody. Some people are much more prickly than that. They don't feel like mop heads at all. They feel they need to use other people as mop heads as they run around and clean up their life. But these styles are not a matter of good or bad. These are just the strategies we use to operate the substitute life we've developed to try to feel safe in this world.

A substitute life is often a life built to achieve a good-looking result on the outside. But underneath, it feels hollow and empty, unsatisfying. Sometimes I see it particularly in young women. They're charming. They're "put together." They look right; they work hard; they have a partner whom they seem to care about. They do right with their kids, and they're just stepping along in their life. It looks good. And it may be good. But I've learned to be suspicious. People are not usually the way they look. Underneath all the "togetherness," there is often loneliness and a blah-ness in people. They are living the substitute life that they learned to build. From morning to night, they build it and build it and build it, by every action, every conversation, and every little piece of whatever they're doing.

On the other extreme is someone like Ted Kaczynski, the math professor who became known as the Unabomber after killing three people with homemade bombs he sent through the mail. For most of his life, he was bright, engaged, getting his work done. But his false life, his substitute life, was already in place. He became more and more withdrawn and lonely, spinning a world in his head which had no relationship to reality, leaving him where he finally ended up. It's not that different than a person who's building a successful substitute life as a tech executive. It may look different, and of course, the results are more lethal in the case of someone as extreme as Kaczynski; I'm not belittling that. The mechanisms are, however, the same.

Whether the result of our substitute life is extreme or more mundane, it is still taking us away from ourselves. It can look as simple as the person who is overactive, over-busy, working hard, doing ten things at once. It's fine to be busy. But, in this case, the substitute life is building a cover of being a busy, effective person so we don't have to face our real life.

The real life is the one we don't ever want to face. We don't want to face that place where we're stuck, hurt, and miserable. We certainly don't want to just rest in it. Instead, we cruise right along. We all have our little drugs, our ways of staying in our substitute lives. Because the desire for something that feels good is so strong in us, the discipline of practice can become, if we're not aware, a substitute life in itself.

Zen practice can be used to avoid dealing with people or messiness or anything we don't want to feel, and thereby turn into a substitute life. Of course, I think sitting is the simplest and most direct approach to experiencing life. But the purpose is experiencing life, not sitting. Some of the finest people in the world have never heard of sitting.

Whether it's a religion, busyness, relationships, or whatever it is, if we use it as an excuse not to feel, we're not living our real lives. We go on with our substitute life, and it never feels right; it's not satisfying. To some degree, we all do this. Every time we feed our substitute life, we cultivate unease, depression, and illness. And yet, at any point, in any day, we have the opportunity to sit and experience our true lives.

When we sit, we begin to know things about ourselves we never knew before. We can see how we've built up our substitute life. We begin to sense how we're always thinking about certain things and pushing for certain things. We feel the body tense up. When we sit every day, that information is being given to us. Every day, if we sit, we see exactly where we're at. That's why sitting is so precious. It's the one time in the day you can really be yourself and see what goes on. And, of course, the reservation there is that our substitute life doesn't want to see what goes on. It's frightening to see what goes on. So, we tend to withdraw or not sit. Part of a sitting career is to begin to see how you avoid your practice. That goes on all of our life. We like our substitute life, or we think we do. It's only when we stay with it long enough that we sense the emptiness and the pain underneath.

The Point of Living

People sometimes tell me, "My life doesn't matter," or "I don't see any point in living." To me, these beliefs point to an important part of practice: to be able to connect with all of life and be there for yourself and for others. That's a major thing to do. Your life matters totally. It matters aside from specific accomplishments in the world, which are fine. But the most important thing in practice is the development of a more genuine person with all the complexity that each one of us is. A stable, powerful base emerges because you're connecting with life itself.

Practice is a long twisting road. There are times it seems wonderful. There are times when it's absolutely boring, difficult— at least for the person doing it. From their point of view, it's unrewarding. Sometimes, you just don't see the point. If you wait six months or a year, you'll see it, but we have to have that kind of overview. Practice isn't a weekend seminar. You can have wonderful insights. "Ah, wonderful, wonderful, I get it now!" Six months later, you may not get it at all. It may be a mess. But that's the wonder of a practice life: the ins and outs, the resistance and confusion. As long as we think the aim of practice is comfort, pleasure, and being calm, we miss it.

In the long run, people who practice are calmer—but that's not the point of practice. The point is to begin to contact yourself as you are: angry, resistant, depressed, phony, whatever you are. A lot of us want to practice just until we hit the hard stuff, and then we go around it. You're not practicing in a way that will fully benefit your life until you pause once in a while at that point of difficulty and just stay with it. Is there anybody here who wants to do that? I don't think so. I don't. But whatever stage of life you're in, as you learn to go right into and through the hard spots, that's what makes your life satisfying.

So, I'm trying to have us look at the fact that a sitting life is immensely rich. It's a struggle. But, taken as a whole, people who stay with it have lives that begin to make sense to them. That can include their trials, their difficulties, and their illnesses. But their lives have a certain base that is valuable to them and valuable to others.

Cutting Off the Escape

SO MUCH OF our practice is noticing, noticing, noticing what we do. You won't notice it all because some of it we don't yet have any idea about. But we'll notice something. We notice the string of thoughts that continually arise when we sit.

Not all our thoughts spring from our core belief or its anxious attendant, our basic strategy. Sometimes we are just noticing a car going by and thinking about that. But usually, even if we are just thinking about what to have for dinner, our thoughts are flowing out of the core belief. When we've labeled and noticed certain thoughts repeating hundreds of times, those strings of thoughts that were designed to fix or change the fact of our experience are no longer so interesting. Something begins to dawn on us, and we start to know ourselves as we never have before.

But there's no guarantee this will happen. Unfortunately, we usually want to escape from ourselves and get on with seeing if our basic strategy can figure our life out. The discipline of sitting still, done diligently, cuts off that escape. When you cut it off, you're left with a direct experience of life. It's a very different thing from not having that direct experience. A life that has a little bit of that every day is very different than a life that has none.

Resting in Sensation

What we need to do—but what we really don't want to do—is return to the pain of our core belief. I'm using the word "pain" because we know it that way, but it's really just a physical sensation. It's not going to kill you. Suppose you feel you're never able to succeed: you're a failure. What does it feel like? We don't want to rest in that feeling. The core belief says, "You're wasting your time. You need to be out fixing the world, taking care of 'me.'" It is always offering this escape from our feelings.

To begin to rest in sensation is at the heart of practice. It's good to know what our core belief is, to know it's a mistaken belief, and to be able to see what strategies we use in service of that belief. But all that knowing doesn't solve a thing. What solves it is when we return and rest right here where we don't want to rest. We try to do this, but instead we wallow in it or obsess about it. Wallowing and obsessing can be very dramatic, and of course the drama is always interesting—but we should be suspicious of it. Wallowing or obsessing is still thinking about our experience, not residing in it.

Sitting Isn't a Virtue

We can develop the muscle of being able to reside in the pain of the core belief. Sitting builds muscle that allows us to stay and rest, for a moment, in our own experience. That's why it's important. Not because sitting is some virtue in itself. Sitting isn't a virtue; it's just a chance to play with this problem of the self.

You have to be careful that sitting itself doesn't become the strategy. Sitting can be the biggest escape of all. It can become a real hang-up if you are attached to your identity as a sitter or a meditator. A good teacher helps. Someone using sitting as a strategy is not a hard thing to spot from the outside, but we tend not to see our own strategies. I knew one young father who told me proudly how he was sitting for an hour every morning and an hour every evening. I asked him who was taking care of his kids during that time, and he looked surprised and said, "It's my partner's job to take care of the kids." That's not noble. It's just another strategy.

If you have an idea of yourself as someone who has a Zen practice or someone who sits, you have to be very careful not to respond reflexively to everything that happens with, "It doesn't bother me." The fact is, it probably does bother you. The first step is to be honest with yourself. You are whatever you are, whether it's irritated, angry, scared, or defensive. That's what needs to be worked with. Otherwise, you miss your chance to feel in yourself what really is. Zen students are particularly liable to have these kinds of ideals: "It doesn't bother me. Everything is fine. I'm above that kind of issue." But we're not.

I once had a student who kept challenging me about little things. I was fine with that. I told my daughter, "I see what the student is doing. It's obvious why he's doing that, and it doesn't bother me." And she said, "Mom, how do you really feel?" I said, "Oh, I'm mad!"

The Way We Want Things

Our nature as human beings is to want everything just the way we want it. But it's never the way I want it. Know what I mean? There is always something going wrong in relation to my plans for the day. When something isn't the way you want it, there's that little glitch in your self. You can feel it. The body tightens. One advantage of sitting is you get to know that tightening. People who sit begin to sense when the body is just present versus when you have a thought that really throws you. You begin to sense the body tensing, and you get interested in that.

When someone does something that we don't like, it's fine to not like it. But we have a chance to practice with our emotional reaction—our anger, or sense of outrage, or hurt. There's a difference between stopping someone's inappropriate action, which can be a good and necessary thing to do, and acting out of our core belief. If you feel you're fundamentally imperfect, and that feels unbearable, an excellent way to cover it up is to try and control or fix somebody else. You feel other people should be different, more perfect than they are.

If you're usually in a position of authority—in your family or your work—you probably have a greater illusion of control. I have that because I direct this Zen center, and that illusion is not good for me. I need to have part of my life where I'm not in charge. Learning a new skill can be helpful in this regard. I'm learning one right now. It's really wonderful for me because I can't do anything right. It's very humbling. If I remember one thing, I forget something else. Then when I remember that, I've forgotten the next thing. I also make sure I always have friends who have nothing to do with practice. That's a trip in itself. Some of them have no idea what I do. It's hard on the ego.

Your life is right here. As we sit with this thing we don't want to sit with, we have a chance to cut off the escape, learn to reside in our experiencing, and let it be. If we can stop trying to fix it, or change it, or be mad at it, it begins to transform us. We don't have to transform it; it transforms us. We become more spacious. It's as though you have more room around you. Now, this is where you enter a growth that is hard to describe. You will sense, in yourself, as you're practicing, that your life grows increasingly free of judgment. It's increasingly free of your self-centered hassle.

We can't catch it all. We're all busy people doing lots of things, but try to work with one thing a day when you're sitting. It doesn't need to be your whole sitting period, and it doesn't have to be while you're sitting at all. Just try to honestly experience one thing a day that's upsetting you. You don't have to tell anyone. You can feel whatever you feel, no matter how ugly, petty, or scary. We have to work with the truth, or we miss an opportunity.

Life Is Not a Thing

WE EACH HAVE a view about life. "Life is hopeless." "Life is meaningless." "Life is tough." "Life is a drama." "Life is a game, and I can't win." I've never met anyone who doesn't have a point of view about it. Even if we can't articulate it or aren't conscious of it, our actions are guided, even dictated, by our very strong idea of how life is. The reality is, life isn't anything. You simply cannot make life into *a thing*; it has no duration and no space. It never stops. Life is change itself.

Our general philosophies about life flow right through our core beliefs. And we have our moods, which flavor these views. Some people have dramatic moods. Some people view themselves and life as dull things to plod through. To be anxious is a mood. Your true self couldn't possibly be anxious because it's not anything, and "not anything" can't be anxious. But, your conditioned self—the one that we're really living through most of the time—can get anxious or be in a hurry.

We think of our moods as being influenced by our physical condition, by the weather, by lots of things. So it seems. Recently, I noticed the difference in my mood while in Hawaii compared to my mood in San Diego. I decided it was because of the weather.

But the weather, at least at this time of the year, is no different in Hawaii and San Diego. I don't view the San Diego air as soft and caressing; I view it as humid, and I hate humidity. But as long as I was in Hawaii, the whole, warm, damp air was just wonderful. I never minded it a bit.

Boredom Is Another Name for Practice

Everybody who sits gets bored after a little while. You can't look at your watch. Twenty minutes can feel like a lifetime. Look closely at the boredom. For me, my core belief is always feeling that life is kind of a disaster. It's always hoping that something—in this case, Zen practice—will make me feel good. That it's going to fix me. When we get bored, we're really saying, "Nothing is getting fixed here." "This is just kind of dull stuff." "I'm not getting anything out of it." "I'm not getting that thing I'm hoping for."

We expect a lot from external things. Think about romantic love. We often start with such high hopes: "This person is going to complete me. This person will make everything better." Then we're bored or disappointed when the other person doesn't do that for us. We will attach our desire to anything. We can attach it to having the Padres win the baseball game if we're a Padres fan. We can attach it to having the Republicans win an election if we're a Republican. We're always looking for something that momentarily fills us up.

With sitting, pretty quickly you'll start to realize it doesn't complete you. You're just sitting there, and it hurts. Inevitably, the mind that is always trying to figure things out, it thinks, "This is pretty stupid to just sit here." "It's hot; my legs hurt." "I thought Zen was supposed to be all about joy and wonder."

You can be bored if you want. But it's interesting to see if you can notice your boredom and also feel the fear at the base of it. That fear arises because, once again, something outside of you isn't fixing anything.

Boredom is another form of desire. "I want it to be different." "I want it to be other than it is." "I want it not to hurt." "I want it not to be so hot." "I want." We think we need something that we don't have and don't feel we are, so we experience it as want. With boredom, it's often, "I don't want to feel this pain, so I want something to distract me. I want something to entertain me."

To really surrender to pain and to be friendly with it, to embrace it, is probably not what we thought this practice was about. We thought it was about becoming enlightened. But enlightenment is not some tremendous state of being. It's simply being with what is.

When you're sitting in pain or boredom, you go right to thinking, "I really hate this; I really do hate this." We can notice the thinking without getting stuck in it. And if we can stay unattached to the thinking, and just experience the pain or boredom, something bigger begins to surround it. We can't experience the wholeness of life, the sacredness, without including everything. And everything includes the boredom and the pain. You can be thankful when your boredom comes because it means you have space to experience what's underneath it.

To the extent you realize that, you'll begin to be willing to experience everything. If you want what you really want, that gets clearer and clearer. This doesn't mean you like to sit in pain, or with the dullness, or with the heat. But then, there is something that develops in you when you keep sitting. There's a steadiness. And the longer you sit, the more that steadiness takes charge. And that's not useless. Anyone who goes through life, particularly as you get older, faces increasing chances of accident, illness, and stress. You can't escape these things. But if you have a practice, it's different than not having a practice. I don't want to put some ideal out here; that's not what I'm saying. I run for the aspirin as quickly as anybody else, but there is something that develops from sitting.

Anticipating Life

Before we sit, we have a mood, a feeling about what it's going to be like. In fact, it's like that with everything: we're often feeling something in advance of the situation actually happening. This keeps us from being aware or noticing the situation we're in at this moment. When we go into any environment with other people, we're often nervous or edgy. We want to be impressive in some way, so we start figuring out what to say or what tale to tell. That's understandable; you're going to a gathering and you have to talk about something. There's nothing wrong with that except it distracts us from how we really feel at that time. We may feel a little bit uneasy. We might be worried that the other people won't be impressed with us, and we'll be stuck with our own painful feelings. All these feelings about the situation arise, and we haven't even reached the front door. We spend our life doing this.

Most of our life is lived in this space in our mind. We aren't experiencing; we're being pushed by the core belief into moods and opinions. We're busy with a whole world of anticipatory thoughts and feelings before the door ever opens. Say you're going to meet a new person later in the day, and that person is kind of important. You may spend a whole morning figuring out your approach to that person. Maybe you comb your hair differently or you rehearse what you're going to say. Your whole morning is taken up with this, and the meeting hasn't even happened yet. Now that doesn't mean you don't have to get dressed. You do. You can even get dressed up. But your mind is taken up with thinking about what is going to happen before the contact even takes place.

This anticipation happens with practice itself. After a few years of practice, a lot of people tell me, "I'm getting an awful lot out of this practice, but it wasn't at all what I expected." That just happens. Our experiences, when we're actually experiencing them, have very little to do with our anticipation.

This doesn't mean we shouldn't have aspiration. Aspiration gives us diligence and discipline. It's different than *ambition*, which is about trying to get somewhere. Ambition is motivated by our core belief that there is something wrong with us that can be fixed if we can get to a certain place. Ambition says, "I will open the door, and I know what's on the other side, and I'll take it." Aspiration is more like, "When the door opens, I will be there."

Weakening the Core Belief

Now, our true self doesn't know anything about ambition or anticipating life; it does not become busy with thinking, waiting, measuring, or worrying. Our true self is just perceiving second by second by second. It's just being itself and responding to whatever happens to be there. When that millisecond of response is over, it's over. We won't ever be able to be completely without thought or anticipation, but if we sit regularly, bored or not, it weakens this ego process. It weakens our attachment to our core belief, and at the base, it's the core belief telling us what life *should be like* instead of allowing us the space to experience life *as it is.*

When we weaken that attachment to our belief in how things are, we're thrown back into our actual experience. If we're thrown into it directly, then that's the passageway, the gateway, to our true self. This is the most rewarding thing we can do. It's a very edgy life. We may sometimes get a response we like, but you can't count on it. There is no way to count on that. There is no settled-ness or security in a life of practice. You don't know what's coming. But don't worry. Your true self can't worry about anything; it's not capable of doing that.

To see what upsets you is to see it through your core belief. Everything we do and see we immediately label with our perception: like or dislike. Go right ahead and label; it doesn't matter. But this is the work: noticing the feeling or thought, becoming aware of the core belief animating it, and then being with whatever arises, without response or reaction.

Practice isn't about liking practice or not liking practice, liking the weather or not liking the weather. It doesn't matter. The weather is what it is. Our sitting is what it is. Our liking or disliking of it doesn't make any difference. Only the practice matters.

Your Practice Is the Conduit

Some people think when I talk about a core belief I'm talking about something psychological rather than real Zen. But if we have a picture of what the real Zen is like, how is that different from a picture of boredom? Zen is a life that eventually has a transforming element to it. Trying to push to find your true self doesn't work. You can't do that. You can't resolve to be good or to be your true self. That's just another system; it doesn't work.

The idea of the core belief is in the mind, but when you get back to the actual experiencing of that pain with no naming of it, you get out of the dual nature of thinking. There's no subject and object; you're just being. If you say, "I'm going to feel my anger," that's not feeling your anger. That's talking about it. But if we experience that anger, we have to give up our core belief for a moment and just settle into the pain of it. And if we can stay in this non-dualistic experiencing, even for a few seconds, it will slowly begin to transform us.

Over time, we develop our ability to rest in that non-dualistic experiencing for more than two or three seconds. We don't want to do that; our core belief is very dear to us. Until we know our true self, that's who we think we are. We have no intention of giving it up, not at all. That's why practice is not easy. That pain becomes your true teacher.

Out of this teaching, you slowly see yourself and the rest of your life in a very different light. It's not ever complete, but you can be there more and more. When you can, even briefly, experience your pain instead of thinking about it, it changes you. That non-dual state is where you can experience your true self. Your true self is peace, freedom. It's always compassionate. It's incapable of judgment. This true self can manifest more and more over the years. Your practice is the conduit. This is true Zen. That's it.

PART THREE

THE WORK

A War Within

ALL HUMAN BEINGS are at war with themselves. You may meet people all day long who are smiling and seem self-assured. Trust me, the wars are there. How clearly we see these wars, and whether seeing them has any effect on our life, is another matter. For most of us, the war is not even conscious, so we have the usual human predicament. Not everyone is interested in the war. Some people will go to their graves seemingly impervious to it. But if you're interested, the war is where the practice is. You step into the war and do battle.

The war is between the way we think we should be and who we are. We are all caught in the feeling that we should be some other way. Perhaps we think we should be kind, patient, forgiving, long-suffering, charitable, and compassionate. It's awful! I'm not saying the qualities themselves are awful. But to hold those qualities up to ourselves as the way we should be is about the worst way of ever getting to look like that. Maybe we're none of those things, or at least not very many of those things, and then we feel guilty and have to hide it.

The war is between wanting pleasure (or ease or success) and being with the truth that life doesn't care about our pleasure (or ease or success). It will be the way it is. Perhaps we know this intellectually. But we feel we should be more okay with it. "I should accept this." "I should do it." "I should be a good person." "I should be unselfish." How are we really? Just the way we are.

Being just the way we are enables us to transform, if we can really see it and experience it. Whenever you're upset, annoyed, irritated, or moody, the war is on. The question to ask yourself is: "How is it supposed to be, and how is it really?"

Two Sides of Practice

Because we believe we are a certain way, and the world is a certain way, we are therefore compelled to act a certain way. This is the world in our mind, the world that creates nothing but havoc for ourselves and others. We can go to our deaths clinging to this world. We say we don't cling to it, but we're terrified not to have it. Yet something within us—because that capacity is always there—doesn't want to keep living this way. That's one side of practice.

The other side of practice is just being the witness, the observer, really seeing every thought you have—not judging it, not analyzing it, not doing anything with it—just seeing, seeing, seeing, seeing, seeing. And as that seeing deepens, it captures not just thoughts but the body sensations that arise with those thoughts. Here is where you begin to know your body, to know the shades of emotion running through it from morning till night. It's a cool, cold practice, meticulous and precise.

This side of practice takes diligence. I'm sorry to tell you it's no easier than practicing with our core belief. It can take years of practice and patience: being aware and labeling our thoughts day after day after day after day. Noticing what's happening in the body moment after moment. Sitting is relaxing, eventually, but for many years it can also be a lot of hard work. We don't necessarily get immediate satisfaction. You get your true life, eventually, if you stick with it. But because we have so much pain, most of us would rather choose immediate pleasure than our true life. We want life to please us right now.

So, one side of practice examines our core belief, which will pull your sense of your life apart, and the other side of practice is careful, meticulous work. Both don't seem that fun, so why do we practice? Because our true self is there, yearning for the freedom and spaciousness that is our true life.

Staying with the Mess

If you want your life to truly transform, you do this by just staying with the mess. You stay in it. A lot of practice is just sheer persistence and patience with the confusion. And if you are patient, it's as if, in the midst of being in this messy room of your life, you notice you've left the window open, and in comes a little bird of wisdom. It won't stay long, at first. Maybe it just appears at the window, chirps, and flies away. But if you stay still and patient, it returns. If you're hospitable, it might even come and live with you once in a while, for a week or so. And you get a different look at your life.

How is it supposed to be? Our hope is that if we run our lives according to our core belief, it will lead to pleasure. It will lead to satisfaction. It will lead to the life we've always wanted. Then, somebody tells you to do this other kind of stuff: really watch, observe, and feel. We don't want to do that; we've got to get back out there in the buzz of thinking, the endless swarm of thoughts. We don't want to observe those thoughts. We don't want to feel the tensions of the body as we play with them.

If you stay with your practice, slowly but surely, you begin to see what you're really doing as opposed to what you think you're doing. *How is it really?* The struggle isn't pointless. The struggle is, in fact, absolutely important.

Old Buddhist texts talk about having your head in the fire. There has to be struggle in practice. Without the struggle, that slow learning doesn't begin to emerge. That fire refines you as you stay with it. Most of us need at least a little support somewhere, a little help. That's why I recommend you find a teacher, a partner, and a community to practice with. It takes a lot of work to stay with this nasty struggle. It can take a lifetime.

The good news is that since the struggle changes the way you see yourself, the struggle itself changes. It doesn't require as much effort. In this war between the way we think things should be and the way they really are, there are moments of truce. The two sides come together for coffee and cookies, and enjoy themselves just fine. With practice, we don't "win" the war, but we have moments of peace. Then, when the truce is over, we may go back into battle.

But we can enjoy ourselves for a little bit, and these little bits get longer and longer.

We may dread practice, but we value the life that comes out of it. We begin to stop battling and instead experience the freshness of seeing in a much more honest way. A life of practice is the most rewarding, the most exciting, and the most alive thing you can do. But it's no piece of cake.

Grasping Nothing, Discarding Nothing

He did each single thing as if he did nothing else.
—*Charles Dickens*, Dombey and Son

LAYMAN PANG WAS a great old Zen master, born in the year 740. He wasn't a priest. He was a family man who rejected formal practice and sought enlightenment on his own. Once, Pang freed himself from all possessions by loading them in a boat and sinking it in the middle of a river. After that, he and his daughter Ling Chao traveled around ancient China as peddlers. Pang seems to have known every major Zen figure of his time. He studied with all of them and engaged them in Dharma combat, a practice of exchanging challenging questions and answers that was popular at the time. Once, when questioned about his life, Pang offered the following verse:

> My daily activities are not unusual.
> I'm just naturally in harmony with them.
> Grasping nothing; discarding nothing.
> Supernatural power and marvelous activity.
> Drawing water and carrying firewood.

He and his daughter spent their last two years living in a cave. One day, Pang announced it was time to die. He prepared himself and asked his daughter to go outside and report when the sun reached noon. Instead, she rushed back in and told him there was an eclipse. When Pang went outside to see it, Ling Chao assumed her father's place and promptly died. "Her way was always swift," Pang said, and died a week later.

This story probably never really happened, but it's still a great story. "My daily life is not unusual," he says, "I'm just naturally in harmony with it." That sounds easy. I could say to you, "Just go home and be in harmony with what you do. When you run your computer, be in harmony with it. When you talk to your loved ones, be in harmony with your loved ones." Simple, isn't it?

For us, it's not simple.

For example, today, I tried to prepare to give a talk and to do nothing else. I was trying to follow Charles Dickens's description, to do one thing and to do nothing else. I lasted about ten seconds. Then, I had a little itch on my face. Of course, I didn't just scratch my face. I got busy thinking about the itch.

Harmony with the Mess

If we could truly be in harmony with our experience, from morning to night, that would be a lot. I'm not talking about the single-mindedness of fierce concentration, focusing intently on every little thing. You lift a spoon, and you focus all your attention on lifting the spoon. That's self-conscious mindfulness, and I'm not talking about that. When mindfulness practice is misconstrued, we pay very showy attention to the elaborate lifting of the spoon or putting it in your mouth. You can learn something from that, but what can be left out of this kind of mindfulness practice is awareness. I don't just mean awareness of the spoon, but awareness of the whole context of your life at that second, which includes body sensations. How long you have to eat, all that sort of thing.

It's very easy to say, "Just be in harmony with life." That's all very nice, but it's not what we're doing. We sort of know all that. And yet, that's not what we're doing. We very rarely just do what we do. We're nearly always doing one thing and kind of veering off in another direction at the same time.

If we're lost in the mental world of our core belief, we never know what harmony is. What straightens this out for human beings?

In the realm of no liking or disliking, the world is absolutely perfect. We do each single thing with no discrimination. Suppose you're trying to work, you're really busy, and the phone rings. We resent the ringing, because we're trying to work. But the problem isn't the phone ringing. It's just ringing. It's not good or bad.

When we become more able to notice and experience this phone ringing, life gets less rigid. Because life is always changing, we become more able to move with it as opposed to being stuck. Being in harmony means you're experiencing your self as an integral part of life instead of as someone who is opposing a piece of life. When you experience harmony, you know it.

From the material point of view, there's no harmony. From the absolute point of view, it's all just happening so it's naturally in harmony. Harmony can occur right in the middle of a messy situation. It's when we can experience the mess, but not be that mess. It's when we can experience that mess without being ensnared by it.

What's Going On Here?

The minute I sense a little judgment of something or a little annoyance at something—that sensing happens fast now from years of practice—I ask myself, "What's going on here?" I take a long, deep look. Sometimes you can do the whole thing in ten seconds if it's just a run-of-the-mill type thing. As we practice, that ability to pause and to question gets stronger and stronger. It isn't that the problems vanish or your ego vanishes, but the ability to look quickly and to be interested in looking grows.

When you practice with something like that—and we all have something or lots of things in our life like that—then the realm of no liking or disliking begins to appear. And that's the realm of harmony.

We start out believing our judgments instead of seeing, noticing, and labeling our judgment, and seeing what else is going on. When you experience anything, that's the turning point.

It's become quite popular in some circles to say, "You have to really like yourself." I think that's backward. You can't just "like yourself." What you have to see is that you don't like yourself. But the self you don't like isn't your true self; the self you don't like consists of your core belief, with its accompanying thoughts and body sensations. With practice, you move through the tube of experiencing and come out in the land of harmony, of being okay with yourself.

The Courage to Practice

Practice takes courage. By courage, I don't mean being willing to stand in front of a cannon and get blasted away. Practice takes courage because we don't want to move off our usual position. It takes courage to stop doing things the way you've always done them, and make a choice to do something different.

What helps me the most with courage is when I can be really honest about what I'm experiencing, which is usually fear. And if I can stay with that and experience it, it seems to get a little bit more possible to do the work, to do what needs to be done.

No Effort, Tremendous Effort

IF YOU SIT long enough, you'll experience hating to sit, loving it, being impressed by it, thinking it's a bunch of nonsense, and finding the whole thing dreary.

Practice is always the same, regardless of what you bring to it. Whether you're young or old, happy or sad—practice never varies. In that way, it contains us and gives us the space to experience whatever is. It doesn't get in the way.

There have always been two schools of Buddhist thought about practicing meditation. One school holds that practice requires no effort. This is true. It really doesn't. You're just being what you're being.

The other school holds that practice requires tremendous effort. This is also true. To be aware of what you're doing takes tremendous effort. I remember being mad at my youngest daughter once. I was really mad at her, and I just wanted to be right because, of course, I was right! I wanted to say a few well-chosen but slightly cutting things that would just settle it. So, inwardly I had this turmoil: I knew from years of practice the harm my words would do, and at the same time I could sense how much I wanted to do it. But I could also sense that what I most wanted was to be close to her and do no harm. I felt that experience get stronger until I began to see that I had no choice. I had to go over and put my arms around her. Of course, then the whole thing was just wonderful in about ten seconds. As opposed to creating a miserable situation, we created a wonderful one.

The desire to be right is so powerful. Years of sitting meditation are not a guarantee of happiness, or really of anything, but that depth of experience may give you those few seconds to sense what you want most in a situation and to act from that. Those few seconds are why we sit and sit and sit. We're building something that can, in the moment, help us make the choice we most want. That ability increases over time.

Ease and Effort

I find that practicing well takes effort. At the same time, to experience life as it is, without any trying, thinking, or doing, is to experience effortlessness. How are these things both true?

Life is often a struggle. We have things we want to happen, and stuff that we think and believe should happen, that doesn't. We are tired of this struggle, and yet to give up the core belief that is keeping us in the struggle takes conscious attention.

To the extent that I've been living an incomplete life, it requires effort to experience more of reality. Our habit is to narrow down what we think of as reality to suit what we think of as "our lives."

To let the senses, physical reality, and the bigger picture emerge, unfiltered by our core belief, is scary. The effort is our willingness to turn toward the unknown of this moment and stay there. We stay there without *doing* or *thinking* anything. That's where the effortlessness emerges.

Our practice is to be aware of what's going on as soon as we can. Usually for the first second or longer, we get caught believing our thoughts. It takes effort to not hold on tightly to our caughtness. But with practice, the caughtness doesn't stay as long. We know we're caught, and, in the noticing, the constriction loosens.

We think we have to change something, to do something. That sounds like a lot of work! But primarily when we talk about effort in practice, the effort is just turning our awareness to our own experience, and then staying there, again and again.

We talk about effort, and we talk about effortlessness, but really, we are talking about making a choice. What do we have a choice about and what don't we? When we feel hurt by someone, we have a choice to rest attentively with that hurt instead of turning away toward comfort, justification, or even despair. We deliberately use our attention to raise questions. "What am I doing?" "What's going on here?" We ask these questions as a challenge so that awareness can float something up. To ask the questions and leave behind our old familiar way of thinking takes effort. Other words for this effort could be diligence or attention. But what we find, once we turn away from the comfort, with practice, is effortlessness. Effortless doesn't mean nice and comfortable. It just means we are aware that we are allowing what is to simply be. There is no choice here, no straining. Effortless.

As Westerners, everything in our lives is supposed to move onward and upward and become better and more successful. Using that backdrop, we often think our own behavior or someone else's behavior is not so great. We want to change something so we can go someplace different or be with someone different. Our true effort is to go toward an awareness of what's really going on with us.

To be aware, for example, that your body is tense, doesn't take effort. It is just awareness. To be aware of your thoughts as they bubble up doesn't take too much effort. It's just like watching a TV: blip, blip, blip, blip. In a sense, it's effortless. But until we know ourselves well enough not to get caught, it feels like effort to keep turning toward what's uncomfortable and to not fall into old ways of being.

Signals for Practice

If your coworker does something hurtful (and they usually do), your first reaction is often hurt and defensiveness. We focus on what is wrong about the situation or the person. But while there may be a lot of truth in that, for our practice, the point is how we respond. How do we move from, "This person hurt me" to "I am experiencing hurt"? It takes effort to pull ourselves away from the self-righteousness and familiar anger. You have to go back to the body and feel what you feel as the body. It takes no effort, once you have put your awareness there, to experience what you're experiencing.

Thoughts like "He hurt me" or "You hurt me" are signals for practice. How do we let go of the "you" and "me" in this sentence and just start to notice the hurt we are experiencing? That is the teacher here, the hurt.

To turn away from anger, once we are fully in it, takes tremendous effort. Most of us are not capable of it in the moment. This is because we're stuck in our own attack mode most of the time. We may feel like we're being attacked. Our systems are ready to quickly react. With even a glimpse of a pause, we can gradually turn away from our attack mode and toward a quiet present space that allows for a more compassionate and appropriate response.

The wonder of a regular sitting practice is that it helps us be less in that attack-and-defend mode *before* the upsetting situation occurs. So, in that moment of hurt or anger, we have more ability to pause and practice. We are able to come back to reality more quickly. We may still feel life is attacking us, but we gain an ability to notice that we feel this way and return to what is actually going on inside. The strength within oneself to do this is the fruit of lots of practice.

Witnessing Your Sorrow

The difficult thing in practice is always that crossroad where it feels like something is hurting us. We're really hurt, and we don't want to budge. Your practice is for those moments of greatest hurt. You're developing a witness, a way to separate the self that has the ability to witness the empty nature of reality. That ability to witness continues to grow as long as you practice. It gets stronger and begins to take charge. And it takes charge more and more, with more speed and less effort, all the time. Our inherent capacity to experience gets stronger the more we are able to witness.

Life may have seemed easier before we began to feel how angry and scared we are. When we practice, we do feel hurt more, but it's a conscious hurt. We witness our own hurt, and we can sit with it. And in that sitting, we hurt ourselves and others less. Our tension lessens. We begin to feel, along with the pain, some effortlessness.

Effort is not resistance. There's a difference between exerting a genuine effort in your practice or your work, for instance, and the kind of effort we make to resist someone or something we don't like. There's no denying that a steady practice, day after day after day, is very difficult. Fundamentally, we have to know what we want for our life and what we're doing about it. That's the effort. And then, being in that, just being, is the effortlessness.

What Is Practice?

If you love the sacred and despise the ordinary,
you are still bobbing in the ocean of delusion.
—*Zen Master Rinzai*

SOMETIMES PEOPLE SAY Zen practice doesn't work. Well, of course, it doesn't work. The only thing that works is us. Our practice is our self. Practice is about awareness, and awareness is just our own selves. It's not some thing, some formula that you can learn from a book and then do it. It's not a form of calisthenics.

Practice is the act of placing our awareness on what is occurring in this moment as best we can. It is the act of attention to this moment. It is the act of being as honest as we can in noticing what is really going on with us in this moment, noticing that we may not like what's going on, and noticing our thoughts and impulses about what we would prefer to be going on. Finally, practice is experiencing what all of this is in our body, our being, and resting in that. Practice is doing this over and over, thousands and thousands of times until it just wears out. We are the joy, love, and compassion of this moment, regardless of what it may look like on the outside.

Practice is that which enables us to live a life that makes some sense and is harmonious. I don't mean it's something sugary sweet; it's not. But it promotes the welfare of ourselves and other people. When we practice, we pay attention. The more we practice, the greater our understanding is not just of our selves, but of how life works, and how things more or less go. When we have that, we tend to have a life that's more satisfactory. It feels better to us. We like, basically, to make sense.

The act of sitting is part of the practice. It might seem very boring, very ordinary. But the ordinary is just a manifestation of the sacred. They're not different. They're absolutely the same thing. Whether you're working on your car engine, going for a walk with a friend, or taking piano lessons, each of these things, done with awareness, is both ordinary and sacred. When you can feel this duality of the everyday and the sacred, without twisting your mind around it, you'll begin to feel a joy that embraces both happiness and unhappiness.

Our lives seem to consist of a string of moments. I get up in the morning, and the moments just tick off as I go through the day. And usually, we greet each moment, if we're honest about it, with a little twist of a reaction in our mind. And that reaction is: "I like this, but I don't like that." Or, "I'm neutral about it." It's the same with the people who cross our path: "I like them," or "I don't like them," or "I haven't thought about it." Particularly, this is how we respond to the tasks that confront us during the day: "I don't want to do that; it doesn't suit me." Or, "It's okay with me; I'm glad to do that." We live as if we have a little judge that's sitting inside of us, wagging a finger at everything. Now, we're not really living our life; we're just trying to get it all fixed so it suits the judge. We can't enjoy our experience or other people because the judgment and the emotion, this concoction in our head, runs our life.

Our practice enables us to take the ordinary moments of our life—one after another—and experience them without judging, trying to fix, holding tightly, or running away. Suppose I'm a quiet person, and I meet somebody who is noisy and boisterous. My first thought may be, "I don't like her." The judgment has already pushed me into withdrawing. The only thing we know is the fact that we are reacting. Often, we don't even notice we are reacting; we just react, react, react, and react. It probably occurs a thousand times a day—almost constantly. For most of us, the only time we become aware of our reactions at all is when they get stronger: when we get strongly criticized by somebody, or we fail in a test, or we've looked forward to going somewhere and find that we can't go because we're ill. (I just went through that last one.)

These are the times when we become aware of our constant judging and have a good chance to take a look at it. If you're sitting in meditation every day, you have an opportunity to see how your mind works.

Effective Practice

As you continue your practice, you begin to see those thoughts in a more dispassionate form, which means you label them. It's painful and sometimes kind of dull to do that. But, something begins to be learned. For example, I hardly ever meet anyone without forming a judgment. But, having this awareness, when I meet someone, I'm much more aware of my tendency to do that. Awareness makes a difference after a while, and you can begin to soften up a little bit as a person. You're not so quick to put a label or a judgment on just anybody. That's effective practice.

Effective practice has two parts. The first is daily sitting. Until you've been sitting, I'd say, twenty-five or thirty years or more, you can't skip it. We all need it. That's the discipline that really helps us get more skilled at paying attention.

The second part of effective practice is our ability to pay attention to life as we're living it when we're not sitting. This might be very weak at first, but as we practice, we become more aware of our life as opposed to getting caught in it. Maybe once an hour we'll notice we're caught. In truth, we get caught more often than that, but we tend not to see the little things.

We begin to see that if somebody hurts our feelings, for instance, it might be two days before that really settles out, depending on how much we're hurt. It might take months for some people. For people who like feuds, it can take twenty years, a hundred years, perhaps three hundred years. Look at these countries that have stayed at war for centuries. The fixed notion that the other guys are all wrong and I'm right is so strong by now that they don't even question it.

The Body's Intelligence

When you sit, you can feel what true awareness is in the body. In the Bible (Luke 17:21), it is written, "The kingdom of God lies within thee." I don't think that means enlightenment is sitting in a little place in there. I think it means awakening is within you, available in every cell of your body.

When we sit, we learn where we hold our emotions in our body and where we are sensitive. This isn't something you can outthink. You can have six PhDs; it doesn't help. Maybe it makes it worse.

You will gain more from your sitting if you keep it simple. There's a place for philosophy and books. But before you dive into a book for the answer—which, it won't be there—you have to dive into yourself. Traditional Western thought often proceeds as if the body has no intelligence. But the body stores a lot of knowledge. When you feel threatened, for example, the body reacts long before the message reaches the brain. The reaction takes place before it reaches the brain. Our thinking is not the most important thing for our survival. The most important thing is the innate intelligence that lives in the body.

Practice is returning, always, back to the body. Feeling the original pain, anger, or whatever emotion it is that you're trying to cover. Human beings want to cover everything, so we don't feel it. We don't want to go out of our way to feel something that's unpleasant, do we? No. If you're like me, you'll find some way to cover it. But the longer we practice, the more quickly we see what we're doing.

Not Turning Away

Life takes us to a certain point where living with our actual experiences covered over becomes unsatisfactory. Say you get a new car. The minute you get a new car, you have to worry about it. Someone's drawing close to me in the parking lot; "They're getting too close!" The least little scratch becomes a disaster. Everything about that new car becomes a worry, including the bigger insurance. We start to see that there is no outside thing that will satisfy us. There is no object, no relationship, and no amount of money that will make everything better. At this point, practice can begin.

Things don't suddenly get fixed when we sit and pay attention. Practice limps along most of the time. It's confusing; it's messy, it's discouraging. Any good practice is all these things, at least some of the time, because practice is basically a struggle to understand the nature of our experience. It can feel like a violent struggle. It's by no means an easy, peaceful trip.

And the main thing that happens from effective practice—it sounds even worse—is that you just get more and more disappointed with all the things you thought were going to make you happy. These things are fine, but our attachment to them loosens, and our need for them begins to weaken.

The more we practice, the less we turn away, and the more our actual experiencing of life gets stronger. We begin to know who we are. To know who you are doesn't mean something magical.

It just means that over time, as things come up, you know how you are, mind and body, with that. And then you can move on to the next thing. There's no perfection anywhere, but there is more spaciousness. There is more peace. There is more being awake and experiencing your life. These are the fruits of effective practice.

What We Hold in the Body

LIFT YOUR ARM straight out in front of you. Make it just as tight as you can. Contract every muscle. Now, let go of all the tension you can, without letting the arm fall. Let go of everything but the functional tension your arm needs to stay up. Take three slow breaths, inhaling and exhaling. Then let it come down. Pause for a moment and try the other side.

Now, contract your face. Close your eyes and make your face as tight as can be. Imagine you're worried, upset, or angry. Now, without altering the basic outlines of your face, begin to feel the same way you did when you relaxed your arm. Keep your face the same (scrunched up), but let all the extraneous tension out. Notice when you let it all go. Can you hear the sounds outside more clearly? Can you take in more?

It's very rare for our body to hold only the tension it needs to keep functioning. See if you can observe your body during the day. If you have a minute between tasks, take a look and see what tension you're holding. Most of the time, we're doing what we're doing, *and* we've added tension. It may be almost imperceptible or it may be very, very noticeable.

Of course, we need to have enough tension to do whatever

we're doing. If we're holding a cup of coffee, there has to be some tension to hold the cup up, or the coffee will spill. If you're sitting up, you need some functional tension or you fall over. The only time the body is really freed from that kind of tension is when you're flat on your back.

An Extra Face

Life is a very simple matter. We're just doing what we're doing. But we add extra tension all the time. If you stop and feel your face, you'll notice it's usually a little bit tight. We don't need that tension. We have a face; we don't need to have an extra face. A Rinzai Zen master once said, "Add no head above your own."

We're hardly ever operating with just the functional level of tension. Even if you don't know what your automatic habits are, you probably know how they feel. Our unconscious habits and reactions make us rigid. Our bodies get tight. We may even get sick.

Functioning is what Zen practice is all about. Our practice is to function according to the demands of life, not according to our personal agenda for what we think life should be: "I want this." "I'm nervous about this." "Maybe that meeting won't go right." "Maybe they won't like me." Every time you have a thought like that, tension builds up in your body. A thought—*poof!* Tension— *up, up, up.* Nobody who is human is entirely free of it. But, as the need for life to be a certain way eventually leaves us, the tension slowly releases, and we are more and more free. The more our practice matures, the more the body is free of anything but functional tension. It has taken me decades for my body to be naturally relaxed most of the time.

Get back to the body. The thoughts are repetitive; they just go round and round and round. You aren't going to lose a thing if you just let them be for a moment. They'll all be back.

Transforming Pain

Our difficulties are so important in our life. They remind us to pay attention. When something hits our life hard, it goes through our body like a jolt. We feel some discomfort. Our true experience is in there, but it's mixed up with our opinions, judgments, and worries concerning how it should be.

Someone who was new to sitting practice once complained to me, "This practice is not making me feel good." If you need something to make you feel good, practice is not much help. But if we just experience the pain, without thinking and overthinking, the pain transforms. Nothing stays painful forever. Not at all. And when we experience the pain and the challenges fully, they don't stay as long. They lessen. Because so much of our pain is in trying *not* to feel it.

When we experience that pain without thinking, judging, or hiding, then it begins to slowly fade. It changes. If you get your mind out of the way, the pain can start to dissolve. It opens up, and finally it just disappears. It's a different way of living. It takes a lot of daily sitting to keep the courage available to do this kind of work. The discipline, the bravery, and the consistency of sitting regularly builds our ability to experience our true lives.

How do you stay with the pain? You stay with it as long as you can, and inevitably, you'll drift off. You might stay with the pain for two or five seconds at first, and then you'll drift—because you want to drift. But when you do it and keep sitting every day, the ability to stay with it increases, and sometimes, all of a sudden, you'll find you're staying with it for ten or thirty seconds. When you get up to thirty seconds, it's a different world. And it's not a matter of virtue whether you stay with it or not. It isn't good or bad. We do the best we can; that's all we can ever do. Nothing we do is wasted if we're aware of it.

Thoughts and Sensations

Nobody likes anguish. But the idea that there's some other way across the bridge from unreality to reality besides going across it is really an illusion. Americans are good at unreality. Our whole culture is based on trying to alter our reality. It hurts—well, go buy a new dress. It hurts—get a new partner. It hurts—take a pill. We have dozens and dozens of ways to cover that hurt. And, because we live in a society that has so much stuff, in general, those ways are much more available to us than to people in earlier or less affluent societies.

Even for practitioners, usually when we're feeling some hurt, the mind is going, "It's so bad. I'm suffering so hard. It shouldn't be like this for me. And oh, yes, I'm experiencing it." That's not experiencing—that's thinking. When we label our thoughts and go back to the body, we are actually splitting off our thinking so we see it's just thinking. When we do that, we're able to see the difference between thinking and sensation. If somebody hurt my feelings, my body gets rigid. My face gets tight. If I just stay there, I may able to notice the difference between my thoughts and my sensations—and this is the path that alleviates anguish.

I use the word *anguish* because that's how most people think of it when they are completely caught up in their thinking-based resistance to reality. In the way I use that word, experiencing cannot involve anguish because there's no thinking. And that's a very important difference.

One reason to sit every day is that sitting can develop our ability to separate thoughts and sensations. For most people who haven't practiced, achieving this separation is almost impossible. They don't know what it means to stay with just the experience. They're always mixing their sensations up with their thinking about the other person, about what happened, about what's wrong. That's the drama. If you don't sit every day, you're really not doing yourself any favors. Sitting is what builds that ability.

Sitting can be very stark and plain some days. I have that thought, and I have that thought and that thought and that thought. I just return again and again to whatever is going on. You just do it and do it and do it. There's an inward shift, a maturing that takes place that enables us, when something really does happen in our lives, to do this kind of practice. For the person who doesn't practice regularly, you think you're dealing with anguish. But you're not. You're dealing with thoughts plus body sensations.

Look at the thoughts first, and then just stay with the body sensations. Then you can't use the word anguish. If I poked my hand, it would be painful. It's only when I add commentary— "Oh, isn't this awful? You know, this shouldn't be happening to me."—that the sensation turns to anguish. Otherwise, it just is what it is. I still take care of it. I still ease the pain. But I'm not in anguish.

Everyone Is Practicing

A LOT OF people do something called meditating. Meditation can mean three hundred things, but we have to understand what the process really is or else we won't have the courage to truly do it—to make our way back to that place where we don't want to be.

Everyone is practicing. It doesn't have to look like sitting. There's no difference between sitting and scrubbing the kitchen floor. I mean, if you truly scrub the kitchen floor, that's being in the moment with what's there. So, we're just talking about finding some way of bringing yourself back into the present moment. Sitting isn't just sitting. Sitting is every moment of your day.

Sometimes we don't want to sit because there is a lot to feel, and if we don't sit, we think we won't have to feel it. But it's the practice of returning to sit, whether we feel like it or not, that builds the container that can hold all that we are experiencing.

Sitting is your best friend. You don't want to look at yourself. Maybe you think you're just horrible. But your best friend is running around with a mirror and saying, "Here, look. Here, look." And, of course, as fast as your friend comes after you, what do you do? You run away. Then he's after you some more. Of course, we want to avoid the whole thing. The core belief's whole project is to try and look good and to avoid anything that threatens it.

If you don't want to sit, walk to the place where you're supposed to sit, and just stand there and see all the thoughts that run through your head, and feel all the body sensations. Then, if you still don't want to sit, don't do it that day, but at least continue to approach your sitting spot, day after day. Don't avoid the place. And eventually, maybe, you'll just get tired and sit down.

Concentration Allows You to Show Up

Sometimes, when we notice we're resisting sitting, it helps to start with concentration. That means to count your breaths or work on something like the koan MU, or a mantra if you know one. All those are concentrative practices because they shut out the world and help pull you into a steadiness.

If you find yourself in a moment of sitting that feels particularly difficult, or one where you just can't settle down, count your breath. Try to count to ten with your breath without losing focus. Most of us simply can't do it. If you think you can count to ten, you're fooling yourself. It means you're not maintaining that absolute, sharp concentration that will show you that the mind wants to think and wander. It's not bad that your mind thinks and wanders, but it's good to be able to notice that. To get to three is a pretty high number if you're really doing this practice.

Counting the breath for the first few minutes of sitting can be useful in a challenging moment of practice, but counting can't be our whole sitting practice because it lacks the acute awareness of everything. We are trying to build up our acute awareness of mind and body, and having a specific focus on counting, while useful, can also keep us from fully noticing what else is going on inside, if carried on for too long.

Concentration allows you to show up wherever you are. It gives you the ability to be aware. We can't be aware if we're also doing something else. This is why I talk so much about the core belief, the psychological and emotional part of practice. We spend most of our lives thinking we're doing something called "living" or "practice," but what we're really doing is devoting ourselves to our core belief. The Zen priest Yasutani Roshi said a student once criticized the fact there was a Buddha on the altar that people bowed down to. The student thought it indicated a false belief. Roshi replied, "I don't worry too much about the Buddha on the altar. What I worry about is that false Buddha within yourself that you bow down to." He was talking about the core belief we each have that we seem to hold sacred.

On Trauma and Posture

We can't separate our body and our self. There is no difference between the two. The way our body is, so is our self. When you sit and feel the body as part of your practice, you're developing the capability of sitting with major trauma. How we sit can either help or hinder our healing.

Sitting is a set of conditions that we agree to because they serve us. They make us more awake. The point of good posture isn't so we can look fancy. It's so we can be erect and balanced, and be a container for all that goes on while we sit. Our tendency is to cover our life. When we sit, we do this by slumping. Sometimes imperceptibly and sometimes a lot, we slump.

A slump is the physiological manifestation of our core belief. We sit up straight because we can't really maintain this same depth of attachment to the core belief when we're not holding the physiological manifestation of it. And one of the ways that we just persist in maintaining this core belief is to slump. We don't want to move up and out of our slumped posture, even though it's holding us in misery.

Slumping is another way of avoiding the mirror our friend is holding up. The mirror is just saying, "Wake up. Stay awake. Stay awake." It's not saying, "Be a certain way."

The Dignity of Stillness

When you sit, try to sit still. I don't mean just sit still enough that no one can tell you're not sitting still. I don't mean wiggle your toes in such a way that no one else can tell. I mean, it's important to really sit still, without tension or rigidity. Just be still. When you do this, you create a container for yourself in which every movement of the mind and body becomes obvious. This extreme state of quiet is like polishing the mirror so that you can see most clearly.

If you're in pain, by all means, move. Moderate discomfort is your friend because it keeps you awake. But if it becomes painful, just quietly and slowly move into a different position. Just do your best; that's all. Some of us have more physical problems than others. That's quite fine. If you need to, you can meditate flat on your back. Sitting is not an endurance contest. You don't win brownie points for sitting in some rigid, perfect way. Sit in a way that serves you. But find a position where you can rest in the dignity of stillness.

A Good Practice Destroys Itself

The discipline and structure of a sitting practice allows us to sit with the dignity of stillness. We want to think about something. We want to go back to our strategies. Just being in the stillness and the quiet, just doing that, may be one of the hardest things we've ever done.

Sitting is not some cut-and-dry procedure. We hardly know what we're doing when we're sitting. Yet, all sorts of things appear. Little wisps of this and little wisps of that; odd bits float by. Sometimes it feels like confusion, and sometimes it doesn't. All of that is part of the exploratory opening-up process. And it's all valuable. Eventually, we begin to sense what all this is.

When we sit, everything comes up. Sooner or later, if you sit, there's nothing about your life that doesn't show up somewhere. I don't think we ever bypass anything. I'm talking about these long periods in practice when, in a way, you're just practicing.

You think nothing's happening, but you grow stronger. At, first you're like a swimmer who starts with swimming one length of the pool and feels exhausted. But an accomplished swimmer just goes back and forth, back and forth. Your muscles grow. When we sit like that every day, when life begins to hit hard, then we have some strength. We know what to do.

Anything can be both the mirror and the avoidance of the mirror. We can misuse anything. We can misuse erect posture; we can misuse slumping. We can even misuse stillness, if we focus too deeply on absolute stillness such that we don't have to notice anything else. But sitting still, with erect posture, is one of the things that's helped me be the most aware of my core belief and how it shows up in my body. So, bring a mirror to your sitting practice.

Practice, if you get right down to it, is very self-centered. We want to get somewhere. A good practice, if you keep doing it with any awareness at all, is self-serving. But when you do it, something else happens. It begins to eat up the illusions that are making you do it. A really good practice destroys itself.

The Way Things Should Be

Our claim to own our bodies and our world
Is our catastrophe.
—*W. H. Auden, "Canzone"*

WE THINK THE goal of practice is to be something like "enlightened." We think we shouldn't be angry, we shouldn't be impatient, and we shouldn't be greedy. Even if we practice regularly, we think we shouldn't be these things. Now, it's nice not to be those things—no one wants to walk around feeling angry all the time—but feeling those things is not the problem.

My Catastrophe

The English poet W. H. Auden says, "My claim to own my body, my world, is my catastrophe." Claim implies possession. Suppose there were no claim to anything. The less you claim as your own, the less upset you'll get. If there's no claim, there's no anger or upset.

What might we have if we didn't have a catastrophe? We might have a shift, a transformation. But if we want that shift, we have to do the work that goes along with it. And some of that work is dull, unspectacular. It's "the same old thing." But if you don't do the work, you have a first-rate catastrophe. You can have a lot of money, a lot of this, a lot of that, and you've still got a catastrophe. Now you may not know it's a catastrophe, but you know that something isn't satisfying, and that no amount of staying busy and no amount of money, can satisfy you. If you don't stop, you'll always just want more. But when we sit, we can notice what we're grasping. We can notice what we're claiming ownership of. We can learn an awful lot from this noticing. When we're not living our life in a way of integrity, we know it. We don't need someone to tell us. But we do need to pay attention.

The essence or core of why we're here on Earth is to learn. And the habit of claiming keeps us from learning. As soon as we begin to think, "This is mine and it should be a certain way," or "It was unfair," we begin to feel disappointed. If you have no claim to own your body and existence, what difference does it make? Can you imagine a cup of water falling to the ground and saying, "It's so unfair"? But we human beings, because we can think and overthink, tend to hold tightly to things, and then there are catastrophes. Our ability to think, to ponder, to analyze, to reason—it can be wonderful. But it can also get in the way of us learning and experiencing life. If the cup shatters, it just shatters; that's all.

What Claim Are You Making?

My catastrophe isn't what somebody did to me, it isn't whether I've been cheated, and it isn't what my lover is saying or doing.

It's only my claim that I should be a certain way, and that part of my world, including whomever I'm worried about, should be a certain way. We all, without exception, make these claims. As we practice, we just become more aware of them.

What is your way of seeing your claim? What are your ways of practicing with this claim on life when you're working? When you're raising children? When you're in any relationship?

When I question our claim to our bodies, I'm not in any way, shape, or form saying not to take care of our bodies. It's just as if you buy a car; if you want that car to serve you, you certainly have to do certain things to it at intervals. Of course, we have to take care of our bodies and take care of them well. But that's very different from the delusion that we have complete ownership or control over our bodies and the things that happen to them. When we think we are separate from everything else—that there is anything that is just us, unconnected from everyone and everything—there is suffering. Because the nature of things is connection. We may not see that, but the minute we violate that oneness, that is a catastrophe. And we do it all the time.

What makes us rigid and fixed is the claim that things have to be a certain way, whatever way that is, and that we, as individuals, have control over how things are. Claim is very possessive. Of course, there is no moment in life that's the same as any other moment. But when we're busy with our claims, we like to get everything fixed so it won't interfere with what we're really doing, which is trying to fulfill our picture of how life is supposed to be. We don't want things to vary from that picture.

So, what can we do? When we sit, or pause, we can watch our claims try to assert themselves. We can start to be aware. The minute there's awareness of the claim, the claim has vanished. Then we can begin to feel and experience, and then we get curious. Sitting in meditation trains your entire being in awareness.

The Same Old Thing

The other day, somebody asked me about the upcoming *sesshin*, "Are you going to have us do something new and different this time?" I said, "Well, I hope not." Sesshin is a formal Zen sitting practice retreat. Each day, the sitting can last six to eight hours. It's very rigorous. Without being stiff, you try not to move your body. Even your tongue, your fingers, or your toes. And it should be the same old thing. Of course, we'd like some excitement. But one of the reasons formal sitting meditation works is because the schedule is monotonous. That enables it to serve you. If you get too fancy about sesshin, if you say too much, it works less well.

How does it work? When I sit long hours, enduring whatever I endure, enjoying whatever I enjoy, but just sitting there, what becomes clear to me is that 99 percent of what I'm doing is trying to claim the world and my body for myself. These thoughts that buzz endlessly—you can call it identification or whatever you want. The buzzing thoughts support my claim that life should go my way. It should give me no pain, no difficulty, no disappointment, nothing that I don't like. That's my claim. And when Auden says "our world," he means that part of the world that I think of as "mine." This usually means the people close to me, my own family, my friends, sometimes my town or city. And, for some people, my country. My claim to own my body and my world is my catastrophe.

I live in San Diego, and when the local football team, the San Diego Chargers, got to the playoffs one year, the whole city went crazy. There was tooting and noise and people running up and down the streets all night long. I'm a sports fan, so I was excited too. We like to take on something and make it our own. Then we can become very excited about it. What are the Chargers to most of us? Highly paid professional athletes. If they get offered more money, next year they'll probably go someplace else. I'm not saying that's wrong, but this emotional buildup we put around anything that we've decided is ours is our catastrophe.

Now, most of the time when we sit, we're seeing our desire for ownership on a smaller scale. We begin to bargain: "I'd just give anything if my knee didn't hurt this much." We begin to compare: "Does anyone else's knee hurt as much as mine?" This matters less to us than our own suffering. What happens in the rest of the world—the famines, the wars, the distress, the living conditions—rarely keeps us up in the middle of the night the way *my* self, *my* family, *my* house, *my* car, or *my* whatever does. I'm not saying not to take care of those things; that's not what I'm saying at all.

When we sit long hours, then the truth begins to dawn: I like what pleases me, and I don't like what doesn't please me. And that will vary all through the day. Our anger is often about the feeling that something is assaulting some part of the world that I think is *mine*: *my* body, *my* world, *my* time.

When we can sit through the boredom, the pain, or whatever comes up, something happens. It's not that we cease to see things the same way but it's as though there's now a space around it that doesn't push at us quite as hard. We soften up. That tight rigidity about holding on, which we all have to some degree, loosens a little.

It's Not Fair

Students tell me, "About six things have gone wrong today: the weather, my promotion, my kids. I don't get why the world has it in for me. I try hard." The key part is, "I don't get why the world has it in for me." This is a variation of the question a lot of students ask: "Why does everything go wrong for me?"

For most of us, life is a personal drama. "Why is it happening to me? I'm a good person. How come? Why is the world doing this to me?" With a question like that, the world comes to an end. We've blocked it off. There is no reason. It's just happening.

A major cause of delusion is that we think the environment causes our reactions. We think they're inevitable. If a certain thing happens or if somebody is a certain way, we think we must have a particular reaction to it. We're actually kind of proud of how we react to it. We like our reactions. We think of the world as separate from ourselves: it's the world out there against me. So we try hard and then expect praise or a reward. When we don't get it, the world doesn't feel fair.

Most people—not all—feel that the problem is their emotions. We have emotional reactions to life as it unfolds. It doesn't suit us; it's not fair. "I was already sick. How come I'm sick again?" *It's not fair.* "Other people don't have these kinds of problems." *It's not fair.* The most common saying in the world: it's not fair.

"My partner/teacher/parent/child/friend/coworker shouldn't be the way they are; they're not being fair to me." To understand how to work with that, even just to be willing to work with it, is not easy. Life is neither fair nor unfair. It's the way it is. However, because we run our life out of emotion, it can feel like getting slapped a lot of the time. Life is hitting us, and that hit is the practice point.

What afflicts us most are variations on our sense that things are unfair. "I don't want to be bothered with the details. It's boring." And I have emotion about all of that. Resentment. That's not real emotion. That's just my mind working overtime. What would it be like to have a life free of that stuff? I don't know. Nobody is completely free, but there are differences.

Think for a moment: What do we do with a sentence like "It's not fair"? What do we do with that? Do we even want to do anything with it? We have to give up our whole drama about being a victim of life, being treated unfairly, and therefore being entitled to lots of things.

You may have the thought "It's not fair" in your relationships. I haven't yet encountered a relationship that's fair. It's not the nature of relationships to be fair. Did you think they were supposed to be? Relationships aren't "fair." They're teachers. But when our struggle is to make life fair, what does that do to us? What happens?

Suppose life circumstances put you in the place where you have to care for an invalid, and this invalid is a difficult person. So, there's nothing but difficulty from morning to night, and no matter what you do, it's not enough. A long, ongoing relationship is such a good teacher. You're not going to be with this person for just a week. That's why romantic affairs work so well, you know. You just get rid of them before you've been around them too long. A relationship that you can't just discard when it's no longer easy is the most wonderful teacher. In a long relationship, there are a lot of little things to practice with. And little things are what practice is made of. I always say that it's a good idea to practice with smaller things so when something big comes along, we have some idea of how to practice.

When we get upset, it's not that something is upsetting us. It's that we've gotten caught on a little hook—the idea that life is not fair. In truth, nothing upsets us except ourselves. When circumstances happen that we don't like, we get upset. Our life narrows. We don't see anything or anybody accurately anymore. We have tunnel vision. In an unhappy relationship, it's rare that either party would think they are the one being unfair. What I think is fair often isn't what someone else would think is fair, anyway. It's funny that way.

It's reasonable to have boundaries and to speak up when something isn't right. Sometimes we have to do battle. But the important thing isn't the description or even the work you do. It's your relationship to the thing you're talking about. When we play with that "not fair" recording enough, we get stuck. Instead of life expanding, it begins to shut in on us.

When you practice with these emotions, they get unstuck. You can say almost anything to somebody if you don't have any strong emotions behind it. I can't believe the things I say to people. But there's no charge behind it particularly, so they can hear it; it's not so hard.

What does it feel like to be freer of the need for control? What is our experience when it's not motivated by fear, anger, and guilt? It's terrifying, because we have given up all illusion of control. And it's glorious and wonderful to feel the freedom of a truly experienced human life.

PART FOUR

EMOTION

Anger and Other Bricks

I USED TO throw things at my husband. Bricks, even. Actually, I threw the bricks at windows, but I wanted to throw them at him. I'd been raised to be a good girl, no matter what the circumstances. And good girls have a lot of anger, you know.

Because most of us do not know how to pause when anger arises, we conflate anger and drama: throwing things, saying nasty words, all that stuff. The anger arises, and we want to release it. It can't stay inside because we think it will destroy us, so we feel we have no choice but to let it out. Next thing you know, the brick hits the window.

Anger is the battering ram that each one of us has. It's fueled by helplessness. Underneath that is incredulous fear. Our core belief tells us that we need to defend ourselves at all costs. No wonder we want to throw bricks and smash walls.

In a sense, other animals don't use a battering ram. They don't get angry in this same way. They can be vicious and violent, but only for a limited purpose in a limited time, when they are physically threatened or are hunting for food. They don't just go around being angry, unless they've been around humans too long. Only humans have this self-conscious ability to look at the world, make decisions about what we think we are seeing, and to act on these decisions as if they were entirely correct.

But as humans, so often we're tired, distracted, and stressed. And even if we have some idea of not wanting to batter other people with our troubles, under enough pressure, we sometimes do.

The battering ram takes lots of forms. But underneath this battering ram is always some version of our core belief: "I am imperfect, and I should be other than I am." As soon as we solidify a core belief that there's something wrong with us, we'll also have a great deal of anger, whether we know it or not. And because of this, we mess up things at a great rate as we go through our life: relationships, careers, our children. When another person isn't doing what we want, we get angry. When something happens that we don't like, we get angry. And if we're not doing what we think we should do, we turn this anger on ourselves. That is the most lethal thing we do.

Usually, what we remember in a story about past anger is the pain. Because when we're hurt, the learning goes right out the window. We only remember the pain. And out of that conditioning, that pain—since everyone has some of that in them—comes the misery of human life, as we grow up and begin to be able to batter others.

Responding to Anger

Imagine a fan, the kind that moves air around. The base of the fan, the part that doesn't move, is like our core self. When a challenge or difficulty hits this base, it affects the base. This difficulty comes into our body and we react. For instance, suppose someone I work with says something that makes me angry.

Now, most of us are used to reacting to situations in certain automatized ways. We experience anger and then right away we react. And usually our reaction looks like the way we have trained ourselves to automatically respond our whole life. So, it may look different depending on our original survival strategy—it might look like yelling, like running away, like freezing. It may look like tears or self-blame. All these reactions are being run by the old behavior. It's like the fan, just running on one of its few programmed settings.

But if we can pause and feel the anger hit us, if we have a practice that lets us stop and notice what we are feeling, we may see that we are feeling anger. We can be aware of all the blades of the fan, which are all the kinds of thoughts and reactions we may be having. These are all the different ways we could choose to react. But with awareness, we experience the strong emotion without letting the blades of the fan begin whirring. Our core self, the base of the fan, remains steady. Then we can truly experience our life, and we are no longer compelled by our habitual reactions.

Each time we can remain quietly with that anger, it weakens

just a little bit, and we have just a little freedom to act more appropriately in the situation rather than react habitually.

This doesn't mean we don't feel things strongly. Some people think being aware means stuffing their feelings down and not having any emotions or reactions. Part of experiencing is acknowledging when we're really angry, sad, or whatever we feel. Because otherwise, we're just getting into the habitual reaction of stuffing feelings down. All humans are liars. We lie about almost everything, particularly to ourselves. We lie about what we're feeling most of the time so we don't have to feel what we're truly feeling.

It's hard to see this. Because that's part of our basic survival strategy.

We react, because that's what we humans do. But the longer you practice awareness, it's almost as though a pause appears. Somebody is angry with you, or you're angry with them, and you really want to hit them. Or you want to run and hide where that person can't ever find you. But there is a momentary pause before you react, and so instead you practice noticing how you feel. You experience it.

You can notice what it feels like to have the feeling of anger and let it just sit in your body. Stay with it without expecting anything of it. If we can just stay with what we are feeling, we'll have a naturally increasing awareness of the appropriate thing that needs to be done or said and the practical actions that need to happen next.

There isn't a right answer for how to respond to anger, or really to any emotion. There is no right or wrong decision, because whatever you do becomes the next experience for you to feel and notice. We always think we can make a right or wrong decision. It's not really true. Whatever decision you make is your newest place to be, to experience your life from. See, there's no formula in this, no way. Experience differs every second.

Developing Steadiness

When we experience anger, our whole body feels it. Nobody in their right mind would want to feel all that. Nevertheless, we do feel it. All our troubles, our difficulties, and the ordinary joys of our life are spinning along, and each emotion finds a place in our body. When it's a painful emotion, we feel that pain. When we have a stiff and habitual reaction, we feel that stiffness in our bodies. It's a reminder to pay attention.

A regular practice gives us space not only to feel our anger but also to build up steadiness so that when we are hit with the battering ram, we can separate action from reaction.

When we feel anger, we can bring awareness to it without analyzing it or justifying it. Practice is a space where we can be the anger without hurting anyone, including ourselves. In being able to experience anger, and feel the helplessness underneath it, we begin to develop a steadiness.

Steady practice allows us to act, even in strongly emotional moments, from somewhere other than emotional reactivity. Life and other people aren't what cause us to suffer. It's our anger, our own reactivity, that causes the bulk of our suffering.

With practice, we develop steadiness within ourselves so that under the pressure of illness, misfortune, or unfairness, we don't hurt ourselves or others. Or at least we hold steady for longer. The more regular and diligent our practice, the more it takes to shake that steadiness.

Practice gives us a choice. We can do what we normally do with anger, which is drama, or we can stay with the actual anger, which doesn't look like anything. When you do that, there's a new world that begins to open. Clarity begins to emerge. At that point, you begin to see what to do.

True Remorse

Staying with anger is difficult. That's why we often express it so explosively; we want it gone. When something nice is happening, I don't mind experiencing it, and I don't mind if it lasts forever. In fact, I would love it. But when anger comes up, often our first thought is, "How long is this going to last?"

Sitting with anger, we think, "I can't sit here another minute." But we do, and there is something that builds. When we stay with steadfastness on the channel that disturbs us, an invaluable kind of learning takes place. You can hate it if you want—but just to stay there, it changes you.

Anyone who sits, if you watch them long enough, you sense the difference. They're not so quick to get angry. There's a settledness, even physically, that begins to show itself. There's a comprehension of the nature of human disturbance. So, even when it seems some people are doing you wrong, you have some understanding of why that's happening. And you have some understanding of how to react to it in a way that doesn't cause trouble. A revolution takes place.

I don't think we ever see all the harm we do other people. But with practice, we not only steady our anger but also see all the harm our reactivity has done. Our practice is, first and foremost, to do less harm. So, when we see the harm we have done, we have to apologize.

That doesn't mean we condemn ourselves. When we condemn ourselves, we reinforce our core belief that there is something wrong with us. It's a self-centered, not life-centered, action. It's good to see that you're a battering ram, but there is a difference between true remorse and turning your anger inward, battering yourself. True remorse is an emotional response. A false remorse is always mental. Whenever we batter somebody, we can apologize. That's a signpost of practice—the quicker we notice we've hurt someone, the more quickly we can genuinely express remorse.

See Your Complaint

BEING AWARE OF our complaining is an important part of practice. It's good to feel underneath the details of a given complaint for the underlying stance we're holding toward life. Even a lament is just a certain species of complaint—one that expresses grief, distress, and unhappiness. A lament expresses the woe of our life: the way we feel it's going wrong or has gone wrong, the way it's hurting us or that other people are hurting us.

Any place that has more than two or three people in it has complaints going on all the time. The subject of the complaint may very well be legitimate. A suggestion, a new plan, or even a demand may be needed. But these are different than a complaint. A suggestion is an idea for how something could be different or go better. A complaint is a recording of how we feel about the world not suiting us.

Nobody wants to think of themselves as complaining, so we dress up our complaints. We hide them so we don't have to know we're complaining. Correcting other people is one way to hide a complaint. Often, the correction amounts to "You're not doing that in the way that suits me." Agreeing with someone else who is complaining is another way we hide our complaints. Complaining about complainers is another one. Meddling is a form of complaint. Overworking and then feeling like a martyr when no one notices all your great work is a complaint. I've heard complaints that were so dressed up in compassion that you would have thought you had Mother Teresa sitting there. It doesn't matter that you complain; we all do it. What matters is if you don't know you're doing it. Because dressing your complaint in a pretty dress is a form of lying.

We all have things that we believe, the belief-thoughts that come from our core belief. When we're criticizing or being helpful or whatever we want to call it, we don't see it as complaining. We think we're just telling the truth, but it's the truth as seen from the viewpoint of our core belief. We think it's unfortunate that the rest of the world doesn't share this way of seeing. If only they did, then we could get on with making a perfect world. It doesn't look like a lie or a criticism; it looks like the truth to us. That's why practice is so important.

A Complaint Is a Form of Anger

We tend to notice other people's complaints before our own. "Why are they always complaining?" When we can acknowledge our own complaints and the feelings behind them, we see that the challenges in our lives spring right out of our own perceptions. It's true that something is happening outside of us and that it needs to be handled, but the difficulty is inside.

Imagine you have a boss who finds fault almost constantly

and is consistently unreasonable. This pickiness is so constant that you feel you can't stand it. What are you going to do? Our inner complaint is like this boss: "This shouldn't be happening. I'm doing it wrong. They're doing it wrong." The barrage is constant. We try to practice with it, to ignore it, to tell ourselves it's not a big deal. But at some point, we get very angry.

A complaint is one form of anger, and anger—especially hidden anger—keeps the world in a mess. Our tendency is to act out our anger, and that usually doesn't work so well, so we try to suppress it. Then it often comes out as little complaints. There's a big difference between experiencing your anger and thinking you have to put it out there and fix somebody with it.

Self-Centered Action and Life-Centered Action

Practice is never about not handling things but always about how you handle them. If you're in a situation that's causing you a lot of suffering, for your health and safety, you may need to change it right away. You may need to establish boundaries so that you get some rest, some time to regroup. But if you have space, then it's better, from a practice standpoint, to focus on your own reactions to the situation. Then you can begin to see the situation more clearly. One way to tell your practice is growing is that you no longer have hidden complaints. You may have different ideas for ways of doing things, but you are not lamenting and dressing your complaints.

When we're lamenting, we usually either take unskillful action or even no action. You can leave—and sometimes, eventually, you need to leave—but you take your self with you just the same, unaltered. The other person remains just the same, unaltered. Our basic vow in our practice is to do good. When you walk out, your situation just stays the same. If that's the case, you're going to meet it again. Believe me, if you haven't resolved something, life will just make sure you meet it again and again and again.

Because our thoughts are our own position in the matter, if we aren't aware of them, the likelihood is that any action we do take will be self-centered, no matter how good it looks. With practice, if we can see the difference between our lament and the situation at hand, any action that we do take is more likely to be life-centered.

We can't address change on a functional level unless we've dealt with our emotions first. Otherwise, we're trying to create change from a place of anger. And that doesn't work. Because with most complaints, no matter how you dress them, the other party senses your grievance, your anger, and your desire to fix things. It's very different from when you honestly experience your own emotions and then try to work together on something. There are always things that need to be looked at and possibly altered to find a better way to do it. But there doesn't need to be so much emotional attachment to a certain result. Change becomes more of an investigation, an exploration of the question, "How can we do this in a way that's less harmful?"

No Complaints

There's a Buddhist story about a woman named Sono whose devotion and wisdom were respected far and wide. One day, a man came to see her after a long journey and asked, "What can I do to put my heart at rest?" She said, "Every morning and every evening, and whenever anything happens to you, say 'Thanks for everything. I have no complaints whatsoever.'" The man did as he was instructed for a whole year, but his heart was still not at peace. He returned to Sono, angry, and said, "I've said your prayer over and over, and yet nothing in my life has changed. I'm still the same selfish person as before. It didn't work! What should I do now?" Sono immediately said, "Thanks for everything. I have no complaints whatsoever." On hearing these words, the man began to laugh and left in peace.

"Thank you. I have no complaints whatsoever"—this is a practice in letting go. It doesn't mean not to handle life, but you're not fighting its flow. If you're in a turbulent stream, and there's a big log heading at you, you would turn the log aside if you could. But there's no extra tension, no resistance to the overall flow. "I have no complaints whatsoever."

From morning to night, we complain, usually inwardly. Some of us are careful about how we do it because we want to look good. It's okay that we have complaints. Notice them, be honest about them. Be curious about the emotions inside them. If we are honest about our complaints, they can be a wonderful part of our practice. Thank you very much. I have no complaints. Whatsoever.

Nothing to Forgive

ONE WAY TO tell if your true self is emerging is that you feel an increasing desire for life to go well for more and more people. This may not look any different from the outside. It doesn't help you look good. But you genuinely find that your focus is less on your strategy, less on keeping tally on the wrongs that have been done to you, and more on a genuine concern for the well-being of the world.

Most of us have met forgiveness that feels forced or for show. "I forgive you because I want you to see what a good person I am." If you've ever experienced that, it's enough to turn you off from the whole word. However, genuine forgiveness, without any of that phoniness in it, is what our practice is all about.

If you want to know how your practice is coming along, look at where you draw the line between that which you can forgive and that which you can't. Now, there are some things that feel clearly unforgivable: rape, murder, molestation, mistreatment of people or animals. There is no question that those things are wrong and horrible and that no one should have to experience them.

You don't have to like a person or like what they do. That is not the question. The question is: how much is there that you can't forgive? Maybe just hearing that word, *forgiveness*, brings up resentment and anger in some of us. But if there is even one person we can't forgive, our practice is still infantile. This may seem harsh, but it's true. If we can't forgive someone, it's our way of staying separate from them. "I would never do that. I must be a better person than that." We hold on to our feeling of superiority. We are all beginners, including me. If there's anything that keeps me awake at night, it's the people I can't forgive. I can't stop working on that.

So, where do we begin? I suggest you practice with such fierceness that you can perhaps forgive the next person on your list of people who did you wrong—it may be somebody who is dead, someone who is in your family, or someone you have never met. But for every person you can truly forgive, your core belief is weakened a little bit. And you come a step closer to forgiving yourself.

Don't try and rush into forgiving someone for the sake of "moving forward." I have two people left on my list who really stand out. I've been working on forgiving one of them for many, many years. Their name has faded on that list—the potency is a lot different than it was—but I've still got a long way to go. It doesn't matter whether we have a little or long way to go. It just matters that we practice.

So, ask yourself where you draw the line. What will you and will you not forgive? Do you draw the line at anyone who criticizes you unfairly? Sometimes we draw the line at the partner who had an affair, the friend who stole, the colleague who cheated. Usually our parents are somewhere on our list, even if we pretend they're not.

Who is on your list? You can reach a point in practice where things that used to bother you no longer bother you as much. That's wonderful. Forgiveness practice goes deeper. We can't even imagine at first the depth of the endeavor. It takes everything we have for all of our life.

We don't forgive for other people's sake. We do it for ourselves. Eventually, we get more and more joy out of forgiveness. Certainly, other people may get something from your practice, but you don't do this practice so that you can say, "I forgive you."

Nothing to Kill and No One to Kill It

One of the oldest Buddhist precepts is "Do not kill." When we practice long enough, we begin to understand that there's nothing to kill and no one to kill it. Until we can see that even dimly, the shadow of the core belief will still be on our life. When I say nothing to kill and no one to kill it, I don't mean something esoteric. It means having a mind and body that are open to everything. You can measure your dedication to your practice by the length of your list of people you have left to forgive. The more you practice, the shorter the list. The simplest way to look at your practice is the length of your list. Is your list getting shorter? When your list gets shorter, more space is opened up. You can hold more and more.

The precept is "Do not kill," but in a literal sense, we can't walk across the floor without killing many hundreds of thousands of tiny organisms. We can't live for ten minutes without killing other organisms. We can't eat a meal without killing lots and lots of organisms. We are killers. Everything has to pay so that we can live.

Forgiving Our Selves

We think that, as we go through our list, we're forgiving another person. But we are really forgiving our selves. Our core belief is set up to defend our selves. If we get hurt, as angry as we are with the other person for hurting us, we are usually the most angry with our selves. With each person we can forgive, we loosen, just a little bit, that negative belief we have about our selves.

So, the more we practice, the less resentment we have. I have a dear friend whose child is seriously ill. It is tempting to be angry at life for this child's illness. I can say that I myself will never forgive it. But in the end, there's just the situation. There's no need for resentment. For one thing, there isn't something called life to be angry at. For another thing, we're all dying. There's no doubt about it. Is that a reason to feel that life is being harsh? Should we "forgive" it? I'm using the word *forgiveness*, but the practice I'm talking about includes any of the emotions that come up in response to the harshness of what seems to be life.

The Gateless Gate

WHEN WE PRACTICE, we develop a basic vision, which gets stronger over time, as to who we are and what we're really doing in our life. When I say "a vision," I don't mean something mystical. I mean acknowledging who you are and what you want to do next.

I have found that most human beings, particularly Western-raised human beings, feel fundamentally they're worthless. Really worthless. Unless we've been practicing for a long time or are extraordinarily lucky in how we were brought up in the world, most of us feel this. We have our own little quirks that give our sense of worthlessness a personal flavor and style, but that's what it is. We don't want to feel worthless. We don't even want to hear or know about it. It's very, very painful to feel that you're worthless or unlovable. That feeling creates a running tension that we may be unaware of until we sit—and then it all comes out.

Suppose I'm covering this core belief in my own unworthiness by being very sweet and helpful, always available for others. What does that feel like? Just stop and feel it. Chances are high that there's fear and anger in all that sweetness. Most of us don't need to go looking for this core belief as if it's something well-hidden.

It's what you can become aware of every second if you stop and sit. Pay attention: something is there.

Life is never hidden because you're living your life through this body every second. It's always right here and right now. You don't have to ask, "What does Joko mean by that pain? Where is it?" The minute you stop thinking (the thinking is covering the pain) and the minute you stop doing (the doing is covering the pain), you feel it. It's not always dramatic. That's why sitting is so important. As you turn away from your thoughts and get back into the body, you're experiencing your own core pain. It's never hidden. It's always right here.

And as we sit, as we develop the power and sensitivity to watch those thoughts cascade around, we learn an enormous amount about ourselves. We begin to sense—if we haven't already—the enormous pervading tension inside us. Though we may not have noticed, it has been there for as long as we can remember.

Getting Friendly with Suffering

When we are able to notice and remain aware of the suffering within us, a crucial ability grows. That crucial ability is just to be in the pain and feel it as a physical sensation. Rather than fighting with our pain or thinking it shouldn't be there, we begin to get friendly with it.

At first, we might be able to do that for just a second or two. Finally, we can be with it for ten seconds. Very slowly that ability just keeps increasing. And why would we want to do that?

What's the point? Why would anybody, out of all the nice things you could think of to pay attention to, choose to pay attention to pain? You could be eating an ice cream sundae or taking a nice sunbath! Why would we choose to do something that is, from our point of view at least, not pleasant? The answer gets clearer as we sit.

At first, we're tempted to go off into different directions in our thoughts, to talk about being spiritual, or to analyze our selves. I'm not saying we don't need to have some understanding, but the point is, finally, not that. The point is to return to what we've been avoiding all our life. When we can just be the little quivering self that's there in the core of us, the transformation begins. When we are finally able to experience that which we do not even want to know about, that's the Gateless Gate.

And as we experience that core, it changes. Slowly, we dissolve this false idea we have of our self—that we're worthless, we're nothing. We are going through a gate that no longer exists.

The Great Realization

Perhaps you think all this self stuff I'm talking about is fine, but you came to a Zen practice looking for great awakening. What does this have to do with real practice? Where is the great realization?

I would answer, "Great realization of what?" If you're looking for awakening, you're looking for something to wrap up and look at. And you can't wrap it up and look at it because it's yourself. The more your life experience develops and refines this kind of clarity, the more you realize awakening isn't something you look for; it's something you are. It will be perfectly clear to you that awakening is, finally, nothing but being largely free of this self-centered dream that we cook up.

As long as you think something is going to save you, you're stuck. If you're thinking, "If only my partner were different," or "If only I had just the kind of work I'm really meant to do," then you're in the sticky stuckness. Whatever it is, as long as you believe that, you can't get unstuck.

A student was telling me about a small experience she had recently of getting a little unstuck. She was driving and stopped at an intersection to let another driver turn in. He'd been waiting a long time, and she slowed down to let him in, and he very irritably waved her on because he wanted to go across three lanes instead of one. And right away, she moved from this benevolent generosity to "How dare you decline my kindness?" And then right under that was, "Oh, my God. I've been sitting twenty years, I've just come out of sitting, and I'm still like this." And then it went down another notch. It was, "It's hopeless; I'm hopeless." And then suddenly there was a sinking feeling, like an elevator shaft broke, and she thought, "Oh, it's possible to practice here." By that time, the person behind her was honking.

There is no point in life where we don't have this stuff going on. That's not the bad thing. It's not that you're going to reach some point where you've become Saint so-and-so. Very few people are completely unstuck. But, you know, there's a tremendous difference between being all the way stuck and being unstuck 50 percent. Even 50 percent unstuck is 50 percent free.

In and Out of Spaciousness

The minute you enter the experiential, you've moved into another world. This is when practice really becomes Zen practice: when it helps us increase the spaciousness. We can keep increasing it until the day we die; there's no end to that kind of growth. We're all babies. We're just doing something, but it's an exciting way to live. This is the part of sitting where we begin to know, I am not my body and mind. I have a body and mind, and they're important. I take good care of them. But that's not who I am. That's where we enter. Who we are is spacious and limitless. This is the Gateless Gate.

Of course, we don't just get to stay and hang out in the spaciousness. There's not some magic place you get to, and then that's it, you're done. It's not like we're enlightened, we arrived, and we now just get to hang out in enlightenment. We don't do it that way. We get a little spaciousness, and then the next moment we're right back in our core belief, snapping at our kids or stressing about work. It's not that easy for human beings, especially in a Western culture where there is almost constant pressure to let your core belief lead.

One of the great misconceptions of Western meditation practice is the idea that you're suddenly enlightened. Forget it. It's true that if you practice regularly, you probably become very different. Though you probably look more ordinary than ever. But even with regular practice, you will likely be unreasonable and lose your temper and stuff like that. The idea of practice isn't for us to get to a point where we float above everything. The idea is for us to practice so we can fully live. Each one of us. It doesn't matter where you are. There's not some virtue attached to sitting; it's only a matter of your intention for your own life. And as you spend more time residing in your experience, the intention itself will change and change and change and change.

PART FIVE

CONFIDENCE

Meet the Parsnips

PRACTICE PROCEEDS IN stages. We go through one stage, and suddenly we may drop into another. We usually stay in a certain stage for years, and then there's a shift, and our life opens up. What's hard is that those openings occur, nearly always, because of crisis or difficulty. Each stage may have many little crises within it, because the nature of human life is that it presents a small crisis almost daily. But, somewhere along the way, there is a bigger internal shift.

We are all, in one way or another, going to hit difficulties. It may look different in each of our lives, but we're going to hit crises. We all go through great lengths to try and make sure we don't hit difficulty, but it doesn't do any good. It may be a severe illness, a job-related crisis, or relationship difficulty. Or it may be a crisis that happens inside. Sometimes, there is just a feeling of sorrow or difficulty that accumulates within us.

Any practice that pretends it will bring you sweetness and light is not honest. But one thing we gain from sitting regularly is an ability to deal—unwillingly, at first—with the crises of our lives. When we practice consistently and honestly, it leaves us more open, softer, more vulnerable, more compassionate, and maybe a little bit more humble.

I say "a little bit more humble" because that one is tricky. We may look humble, but inside, we're arrogant. Now, when something threatens what we think we know—and a lot of things threaten it every day—we feel attacked. So, we're threatened all the time. If we don't practice for these little crises that happen every day, then when a real big difficulty comes, it's like being dropped into turbulent water even though we don't know how to swim. We have to learn to swim. The best way to learn to swim is to make your daily life your practice. That's when we learn to swim, at least well enough so we can go into deep water and not get into trouble. The very nature of the discipline involved in sitting regularly helps us not to drown. But even though it may save our life, it doesn't mean we want to do it. In fact, we'll do almost anything to avoid the pain and the difficulty.

Think of sitting as eating, and what we have to digest is difficulty. You like most food, but there is one you particularly don't like—say, parsnips. I hate parsnips. But your best friend is giving a dinner party, and a big bowl of parsnips is sitting in the middle of the dining table. Your friend tells you that she's made this wonderful new recipe and you're going to love it. She loads up your plate with parsnips. How are you going to avoid them? Parsnips don't look any better close up, by the way. They look worse. Now what are you going to do?

What we want to do with difficulties is to keep them away—to discuss the parsnips perhaps, but never ever eat one. We'll eat anything else—ants or crickets or frog legs. But parsnips? No way—until we get to a certain point when that's what we have to eat. We get to a point where the parsnips, the difficulties, are in front of us. There's all the tension and suffering that comes from trying to pretend our difficulties aren't happening. At some point, we can't avoid it any longer. But we realize we don't know what it means to not keep avoiding it.

So, we try to pretend. When we can't avoid it, we try and figure out how to fool everybody into thinking we ate them. If there is a dog handy, you know, you can try feeding them to the dog under the table. You can move them around your plate a lot. Read a book about them. A parsnip is still a parsnip. It's still there needing to be eaten. So, what are you going to do?

It's important to honestly experience our reactions. I'm not saying you should try and love parsnips. False-positive thinking would say, "You know, parsnips are really wonderful. I'm lucky to have the parsnips. Other people are starving. So, I will just enjoy eating this." Then you'll throw up. That's not genuinely being with that situation.

If you can't eat it, just look at the little pile of parsnips, be there with it. And in our terms, honestly experience it—feel what you feel within your body. Eventually, the eating will come a little easier. Sometimes we have to stay in that halfway place, where you don't do anything except just look at the problem and see how you feel about it, for a long, long time.

Then, when we can, we take it an eighth of an inch by an eighth of an inch, put it in, and swallow it. And the next time that particular vegetable comes around—"Well, I didn't die from that, so maybe I could do a half-inch by half-inch bite." We work up to it. That's what daily life practice is like: first an eighth of an inch, then a little more, and a little more, and a little more. Our capacity grows. Not that you have to like parsnips. But, sometimes, you can eat them.

We meet the parsnips everywhere. There is no answer except the one thing we have to do. And to understand that is what practice is about: to understand our own resistance, to understand a little bit how to deal with that resistance. And to know that even if you handle the parsnips, there will be something else next.

Self-Confidence

This practice is all about freedom, not for the sake of something called freedom, but freedom so we can function. If you're paralyzed by a hundred varieties of parsnips, you can't move. You're so busy avoiding and rationalizing that you don't have any time to live. You have to take care of one problem and another and another or else you can't live. You're not free. Life feels meaningless and constricting. We may experience this as a vague, constantly unpleasant feeling. Our whole practice is the practice of freedom—not freedom *to do whatever we want* but freedom in any given situation *to be with whatever it is* and the freedom to be able to respond appropriately and with compassion.

Self-confidence isn't something you read in a book and then you do ten things. Self-confidence comes when, no matter what happens, you know that after drawing back a few times and trying to avoid it, you'll settle in. You can digest it. You'll begin to see what practice is and what you might do about it, because it gives you freedom. It's not an aimless thing to do. If I can handle the parsnips, it means I can go to any dinner party, be courteous to the hostess, and eat what is served.

And when you have this resilience and self-confidence, it radiates out, affecting others. If you can get along with your partner, your children will be happier. You may not be doing anything in particular with the children, but if you find yourself less annoyed and more loving and accepting with your partner, the children change too. This is true anywhere. It doesn't mean we eat what is toxic—if a relationship or a situation isn't good for our health, we should leave. It means we can handle anything that's served by life. It means we have more discernment over what we can digest, what's necessary for our health, and what we need to leave behind. The question is, how can we digest in a way that feeds us and gives us strength?

99.4% of Our Problems

MOST OF US have this one basic question: How can I have a life that makes some sense, that feels good in a certain sense, and is meaningful or satisfactory to me? It's a fine question, but why does it seem so hard to solve? Something almost always bothers us. If it isn't people, it's situations, or the economy, or the election, or something somewhere. Or, if nothing bothers us at the moment, there is always the hidden little idea that maybe this won't continue. And it probably won't. We buy stuff, a lot of stuff, and that can be fun for a moment, but most of us who practice are pretty clear that's not the answer.

Being human, with the amazing minds that we have, we begin looking for an answer to this question. We're hoping for some magical understanding, some vision of life, and some great experience that's going to do it.

A Zen monk once asked the great teacher Dazhu Huihai, "What is great nirvana?" The monk was asking the same question we're all asking: "What is the great wonderful answer?" The teacher replied, "Not to commit oneself to the karma of birth and death is great nirvana." The monk continued, "What then is the karma of birth and death?" And the teacher answered, "To desire the great nirvana is the karma of birth and death."

Don't get caught on the word "karma." Dazhu Huihai is just saying to desire this great answer is the great mistake.

But we all desire a great answer. So, what are we going to do? Our life doesn't quite suit us; we want an answer. And the master is saying that just wanting the answer itself is your mistake. Where does that leave us? More annoyed than ever.

I have an old book that I used to pore over many years ago. It's so old, it was photocopied and is hardly holding together. It's by an English philosopher who called himself Wei Wu Wei, for whatever reason. He wrote that 99.4% of our problems come from a concern for the self. And there isn't any self. Another way of saying this is that all our problems are versions of "My self is disturbed by what other selves are doing." And there aren't any other selves.

There isn't a separate self because there's nothing in the universe that's truly separate. From the absolute point of view, there's nothing that's separate. On the level that we live, though, there's nothing but problems. That why it is a great error to be attached to finding the truth of life and the source of all happiness. If we think "I have to understand everything," this in itself is a great error. Because there is no "I" to understand anything.

There's always my "self" confronting your "self." If I were to look at our "selves" closely enough—if I were to get a big enough microscope—I could see that we're made of molecules. But suppose we look with a much more high-powered instrument than that. If we could have a great enough magnification, we'd see that, for the most part, we're just light and energy. It makes scientific sense that we're all the same thing.

Our problems come because at the level on which we live, the material plane as we call it, we're distributed into little packages that look like a you, a me, the guy I like, and the guy I don't like. We have all these packages. Now, it's not so hard to rattle through thinking like that and to see that we're all the same thing. When somebody insults you, it doesn't make any difference at all that on some ultimate level they are no different than you. On the level of the everyday and on the level of the body, it still hurts. That's the problem with trying to attack the human problem from the standpoint of philosophy or physics. You can understand anything intellectually, but it doesn't affect your life. I can say to myself, "He's just a bundle of light and I'm just a bundle of light." But if he doesn't like the way I cooked his lunch, well, I'm still annoyed. The great oneness of everything may be the ultimate reality, but we don't usually notice it very much in our everyday lives.

Tasting or Judging?

What on earth does any of this have to do with our actual living from moment to moment? We can practice in a way that makes inroads into what we think is the reality of the separate self. We do this by just practicing with what is. Leaving all the thinking stuff behind. This ultimate reality is always present in our experience when we have moments unclouded by thought or judgment.

The other day, I was eating with a group of students. One student who has been practicing for a long time asked another, "Are you tasting or are you judging?" Putting these two words, *tasting* or *judging*, side by side sums up the human problem in a nutshell. When we're totally tasting our food, running a mile, tying our shoelace, or frying an egg, there is no self.

As you eat, can you just experience the oatmeal or rice or whatever you are eating? In other words, have you got your mind wrapped around the thing, or are you simply experiencing it? Perhaps you have an opinion of the oatmeal. We spend a lot of time with our opinions.

I'm not saying that for the whole of your meal you have to strictly notice only the food. Just eat and be aware of whatever you're aware of. There's the food, but you are probably also aware of the sounds around you, the temperature of the air. These are part of the experience of just eating, with the whole of your experience doing this one thing.

There is no way to get stuck in the idea of your self when you're just doing something—really doing it. Are you tasting your food or are you worrying, analyzing, speculating, and remembering? Right now, are you reading these words or are you judging? Probably a little of both. Do I like this idea? Do I agree with this idea? Or perhaps you're trying to hurry up and finish this chapter so you can get to whatever else you want to do with your afternoon.

Are you tasting or are you judging? Are you driving or are you remembering what happened last week? Are you planning your class or are you thinking about what happened last time with that class?

Are you listening, or do you already have thoughts about what that person is saying before they've even finished the sentence? The question about listening is a big one, because most of us find listening almost impossibly hard. Are you receiving or are you pushing away with your mind? We don't want to receive; we want to keep ourselves separate and have an idea of everything out there, with our little mind, judging, so we can be sure it's safe. I'll keep you at just the right distance. Maybe it's six inches away, but no closer. Am I feeling my body or am I upsetting myself? The minute you're feeling your body, the minute you taste, there is no self. The minute you're really doing anything, there's no self. No self, no problem.

When you wake up and you've got a difficult day ahead of you, your head fills with thoughts. I look at my calendar sometimes, and I think, "Yuck, just yuck." But I've practiced enough that I do that once and then begin to just feel my way through each thing I do each day, and it's fine. Feeling *yuck* is okay. But do you stay with *yuck*—thinking and worrying and feeling sorry for yourself, which is all thinking born of your core belief—or do you taste the moment?

The Uses of the Mind

We tend to think if we could just settle the question of what life is, we'd be happy. But there is nothing to settle. Isn't that disappointing? There's no matter to be settled; there's just experience. It doesn't mean not to think. You have to think about how to do it, but fundamentally it's just that you have an experiential day as opposed to that day of rushing, worrying, blaming yourself, and finding fault with somebody else. Understanding begins to arise, and your life gets clearer. You don't even think about it; it just gets clearer. Your true self begins to break loose.

The intelligent and good use of the mind is very important in practice. But we often use it for judging rather than for understanding. We use it to see what someone else is doing wrong, to get angry, to talk to all our friends about it, and to talk to our self about it, sometimes for days or weeks.

Suppose you have a good friend and, all of a sudden, she stops calling you. You don't see her at all anymore. I had a friend like that when I was very young. I was just married. We were friends with another couple, and we did all sorts of things together, little dinners or hikes. None of us had kids at that point. It was a nice friendship. We used to talk on the phone three or four times a week. Suddenly, one day her calls stopped. When I tried to call her, I would get no answer. This was before voice mail or even answering machines. If she heard it was my voice, she would just hang up. I was devastated. What had I done? I never did find out, and I never heard from her again.

What do we do when something like that happens? Do you think my big toe starts to work overtime? No, it's not my big toe; it's my mind that returns to the same place over and over again. When this happens, it helps to label your thoughts. The mind tries to wrestle the reaction down to "I'm absolutely right and she's absolutely wrong." I'm not talking about the mind analyzing in the sense of a scientific problem, which can be helpful. I'm talking about this futile thing my mind does, running around analyzing my neighbor when she doesn't return my phone call. Am I experiencing the pain of that, or am I defending and reacting to the pain? Letting the mind run is a way of defending and reacting.

Now, for most of us, when really tough stuff is hitting us, our minds can't do anything except spin. That's one reason regular practice is so important. Even if our life is uneventful and things are going pretty well, we're building muscle. We're building the ability to lift a heavy weight when we have to. Years of sitting help us be able to watch and, finally, to experience the misery we're going through. To be present and be miserable. It's the last thing we want to do.

Our work is to really feel our misery, with no thinking, as much as we can. If we can feel it, without judging, it begins to heal itself. And out of that healing, a measure of understanding begins to appear about the whole situation that you're in. There is a calming, an ability to do something that makes some sense.

Do One Thing

Years ago, when I was working, I always had a sign on my desk to never do more than one thing at a time. If I picked up the phone, I didn't write, unless that was required to take down a message. If I picked up the phone, I didn't open up a drawer. I did each thing: *ding, ding, ding, ding*. It was a training. A lot of training in itself is foolish, but it has to be done until the muscle changes its habit. Training is exercising the mind so it doesn't have so many automatic pathways to jump into. The jumping is what creates this feeling of being overwhelmed. Because we're so used to doing things our habitual way, sometimes it helps to begin with strict training, and then as your muscles get stronger, explore other things.

Another way I like to put this is, "Just do your work." You might start small. Take one meal a day, for example, where you practice tasting, not judging. You don't have your phone or your book, and you don't write or do something. Training in itself is nonsense, because life is fine just as it is, but we're not going to see that without the diligence of practice.

You can create strict practice moments in your daily life, scattered around your week. I had a student who was a heart surgeon in LA who was always a nervous wreck. He was really worn out. He adopted the practice that whenever he walked down a hospital hall, he did nothing but just feel the soles of his feet as he went down the hall. He would just put his attention on walking, with no thoughts of the operation coming up, or the one he just completed. Nothing but just feet, feet, feet, feet. Doing this practice, he noticed with amazement that he was feeling less tired at the end of the day. His body, his whole being, got little bits of refreshment, so he could function better.

We're not talking here about wasting time. In the long run, practicing like this is more—if you want to use an American word—efficient. The most inefficient thing is to be doing one thing while spinning your head about something else.

The Vastness and the Peanut Butter

The apparent universe neither arises *via*, nor
independently of, sentient beings. The apparent aspect
of sentient beings arises *with* that of the universe, and
the universe becomes apparent concurrently.
—*Wei Wu Wei*, Open Secret

THE TAOIST PHILOSOPHER Wei Wu Wei's words are a fancy way of saying that since nothing exists in the way of space and time, all that we see arises at the second we see it. The seer and the seeing are part of the same moment, the same experience of seeing. If you think about this too much, it will drive you crazy. But there is something important here for how we understand the world around us.

My universe—in this second—consists of me, you, the traffic, the rug, the green leaves. All that is part of the apparent universe, which is my universe. For you, it's these words in front of you and whatever else you see and experience. The idea that there is a universe that existed five minutes ago or that will exist in five minutes is just that: an idea in your head. There is only arising, just arising, that's all. Arising has no time, no space, but here it is.

The Third Patriarch of Zen, Jianzhi Sengcan, said at the end of that long and beautiful poem that we read once in a while ("Faith in Mind" or "Hsin-Hsin Ming"): "The infinite universe stands always before your eyes." The apparent universe, and it's just an arising. We'll get back to that.

Zen teacher Maurine Stuart said, "Zazen washes away all conceptual thought and makes the mind clear and fresh." The Zazen mind is the kind of mind that develops from sitting. Practice isn't about playing with these ideas in your head. It's making it real for yourself. If the universe is just arising with no space and time, it means everything that is arising is of equal importance. It means all these things are equally arising—the pain in your leg, the cockroach that's invaded your house, the job you want or just lost. When something's arising, we want to glom on to it, have thoughts about it, and make it solid and real. It's not solid or real; it's just arising. The person you hate is just arising. It isn't that there's you and him and the cockroach and the pain in your leg. There's just what Zen master Dogen calls "whole being." It's not that we're all pieces of whole being; there's just whole being arising.

Our job, in practice, is to experience this arising. It doesn't work to think about it abstractly. We don't experience "the person we hate" abstractly. We think of it as Harriet, sitting right over there. What or who was it today that you didn't think of as equal to yourself? Was it the cockroach? The phone call you got as opposed to the call you wanted? Your lover? Your child? What, at any given moment, do you feel is not equal to yourself? From morning to night, we judge a thousand things a thousand times. If we didn't, we wouldn't mess up things, neglect things, put them out of place, favor one situation or person over another, lose our temper, or have fancy ideas of being a victim. If we experienced it as all just arising with no time or space, we wouldn't be able to do that.

Life and death, receiving and giving—all the same. There's no space, so they're identical. Succeeding; failing. These are words and thoughts projected on something that is without thought. To see everything arising isn't a thought. It's just, "Here we are." And the only thing that interrupts the unity is thinking. If I really believe that stuff about Harriet, she's not just arising for me; she's an impediment sitting over there. Something I've got to get rid of. Do you see what I mean? And so, I've gone from arising, which has no space or time, to a very fixed notion about something. And since we don't do that with just one person or thing but with many people and things, we create lives that cause us difficulty.

It stops me cold when I realize what I do all day long. There are all sorts of things I neglect or misplace. It takes a lifetime of practice to see that there's nothing that's not equal to yourself. You're just arising.

Even in the realization of this basic equality, we still have priorities. We have things we want to accomplish. Some things get put aside. But the attitude with which we do that changes. We aren't sloppy when we're really appreciating what goes on. Basically, our attention is always slipping from what's arising and going back to our notion of our selves. The core belief is our frantic attempt to get life solidified, controlled, and fixed in some way over long periods of time so that we won't get hurt—or so we think we won't get hurt. That's a way of dying. It takes our attention off of the life that is arising in this very second. And we're all dying in that way a little bit. Practice is to begin to live again.

A Little Slippage

My eldest son is an athlete. He's in great shape, and when he visits, he always looks me over to see how I'm doing. Often he says, "Hmm, you have a little slippage there." I love that term, "a little slippage." We human beings are all about a little slippage. When we are not aware of this universe that we're living in, we slip in all sorts of weird ways. We can always see our slippage. For instance, if you lose your temper, if you have emotions that boil over, unattended to, that's slippage.

We all have, in our life, some degree of inattention. Depending on our particular core belief, it will take one form or another. It may take the form of disorganization; it may take the form of overorganization. It may take the form of being sloppy, or of being excessively neat. If you're excessively neat, what is it that you haven't paid attention to? That's harder than the opposite. Have you ever been in a house where you're kind of afraid to move because you might disturb something?

To be excessive in one thing is to ignore something else. I'm thinking of the little mess I have next to my bed. I've been so busy, and as the stuff just piles up, I say, "Oh I'll read it later. I'll just put it down there." Then there's this little pile that grows and grows. Every time I put something in that pile, my mind is racing on. It isn't there.

We can notice a lot of things. I can notice the pile next to my bed. I can also notice that I don't want to do anything about that pile. I'm tired. That's noticing. The more you notice, the more you become aware of your core belief and how it influences you to have a rigid, fixed way of living, so that you will be protected.

When we don't pay attention, we do thoughtless things that hurt other people and ourselves. Any form of unkindness is also a lack of attention. If I'm truly looking at you, if you have my full attention, it's pretty hard to be unkind. I can only be unkind to you when I don't really see you. My mind is caught by my core belief and its one-point agenda of defending itself. I'm too focused on this sense of self to see you. All unkindness is inattention, a lack of understanding. There's just the moment, this arising, arising, arising, arising. That's all there is. There isn't the fact that it arose five minutes ago. That's nonexistent. It's included in your thought, but as a fact, it doesn't exist.

Fear Is Inattention

Often people tell me, "I'm so afraid. Fear is running my life. I've got this awful thought." It sounds terrible. How many of you sit around worrying, "What's going to happen next?"

Fear is inattention. I don't mean that in a judgmental way.

Suppose your dear friend is ill in the hospital. Of course, go see him. Bring a present. But suppose it's Saturday and you can't see him until Tuesday, and you're worried about him. The best thing you can do for him, for you, is to pay attention.

Pay attention to your own life. Focus on your thoughts and label them. Focus on your body sensations and feel them. Do what you are doing. Fear is just thoughts plus physical body sensations. Fear is getting caught, particularly in the thoughts. Your friend is sick in the hospital. This is very difficult. I'm not saying it's easy. You don't serve your friend by just escalating into upset and fear. "What's going to happen? Isn't it awful?" When you do that for a couple of days, you're worn out. You're of no use to your friend when you go to visit. But if you can spend the time paying attention before you see your friend, you're building your ability to be with him and to be with the pain. If you are stuck in fear, you can't pay attention, and paying attention is the best thing you can bring to a situation.

Nothing but the Whole

Emptiness here, emptiness there, but the infinite
universe stands always before your eyes.
—*Jianzhi Sengcan,* The Third Patriarch of Zen

We're not part of some larger whole. There's no us, no fixed self. There is nothing but the whole. Because there's nothing but the whole, there's a lot of space for appreciation. I don't appreciate you because I'm such a good person that I've learned to appreciate. I appreciate you because there is no "you" separate from the whole being. Everything arises together. Buddha nature is whole being. Does that mean it exists? Or doesn't exist? Both would be thoughts in your mind. You can't get too far with words. You get farther with attention to this very moment's experience.

When we come back to attention, we're faced with all our emotions, our fears, all the things that don't go well in our life, and all that we hope will go well. As Maurine Stuart said, "You have your own Zazen mind; just listen to it." Listen to it, receive it, and let in. If you don't, you'll suffer. If you do, you'll suffer less. It's a nice change.

We often view Zen practice as this way of understanding the nature of reality. And we think if we just could understand the big picture, we wouldn't have so many little problems. But the big picture is just a thought. The truer question is, how do we transform in this moment?

To experience the whole requires paying attention to your core belief, your strategies, to the little episodes in your life, to what you taste, and what you are neglecting. Believing intellectually in emptiness is an error, but believing in some other things is a catastrophe in terms of practice.

I remember being at a Zen center once for a long practice period. We were all eating breakfast outside in the fog. It was very early morning, and it was cold. I felt a bit blurry, a bit yucky.

And then, all of a sudden, there was this roar from the teacher: "How can you even think of enlightenment when you don't see that your neighbor wants the peanut butter?" It was fun. I don't have much interest in people who have seen the vastness if they can't pass the peanut butter.

Getting Wet

BOTH AS A teacher and as a practitioner, what has always interested me is the tension between our false life and our true life. Our false life, the substitute life we're living as a consolation prize, springs from our core belief. Our true life is just meeting life in an open, responsive way. Our true life is what we really want. Yet we're always at war between these lives. What makes it possible to turn from one life to another? What is it that slowly brings us into our true lives?

If you've ever been on the beach, you've probably had the experience of walking along the shore—just walking along, perhaps talking to a friend—and suddenly you're wet. The tide is coming in, and all of a sudden there's one wave that comes further. For a while, there may be just one or two waves, and then another wave comes in even a little further. What we want in practice is for the tide to come in as much as possible.

Looking over a lot of years of life, I can say that, for me, the tide never comes in fully. In fact, it might even go out a little bit. As long as I think that something else or somebody else is responsible for my life, then it's their fault. By any ordinary standards, it may be their fault. I may have every reason to think that. But, as long as I feel that way, the tide never comes in.

Victim or Perpetrator

Suppose somebody cheated me and took all my hard-earned savings. I might then think of myself as a victim, in the ordinary sense of the word, but I'm not a victim in the practice sense of the word. These are two different worlds. And you'll never see the second world as long as you believe in the first world. I don't know of any way for that tide to shift except for a person to begin to understand that if you believe yourself to be a victim, the tide will never come in. This shift is so hard to enact because the whole message of the core belief concerns the difficult, imperfect self that I think I am and the constant maneuvers I need to keep making so I can deal with the pain of that core-belief pain.

Practice can help shake our beliefs and our victimization. Perhaps we now buy into 50 percent of our belief in our victimhood instead of 90 percent. Part of the role of a teacher is to accelerate that process a little bit. It's unpleasant, but it has to be done. Even so, some of us are very determined, and we'll hold on anyway, at least for a while.

What is it that leads you to suspect that there has to be another way of seeing things? For many of us, it's that the substitute life doesn't work for us anymore. We try really hard to make it work, and we may even be succeeding with the external form of having it work. But underneath, there's just inescapable terror.

Some of us, instead of thinking of ourselves as the victim, make other people the victim. As long as we're caught in a core belief, we're in a dualistic life: there's me and there's the rest of the world. That view doesn't give us much choice; we have to either repel the world in some way or placate it. We're either a victim or a perpetrator, always doing one or the other. We really think for a long time that one of these two ways of life is going to work for us. And they do work, sort of, but they don't work really.

Perhaps our pleasing of others is going along really well, and we're getting a lot of rewards out of that, whether it's financial, personal, or whatever. Perhaps we get exactly what we thought we wanted. But when that has happened, it usually feels just about as bad as when something falls apart.

It's all right to suffer. It may be your suffering that finally turns you to your true life. You get tired of suffering. Or, as in my case, you see you're making other people suffer. We may think practice is about our own suffering, but when we don't do our practice, other people suffer. That's a very powerful motivation.

You see your own pain, and then you also see the pain you're causing others. When you have had enough of this, your turning to your true self begins. And once it begins, the process will keep accelerating. These are very painful times. A lot of pain arises that you've spent a lifetime trying not to feel.

Sitting Is the Base

We sit because the sitting process itself interferes with our habit of being a victim or a perpetrator. As we watch those thoughts and label them, sitting reveals a repeating pattern that begins to be obvious. We sense something that we didn't sense before. That's why sitting is the base. Sitting enables all those patterns to become clear to us. At some point, the patterns are so clear and our suffering's so obvious that we don't have any choice. We reach a point where we have to sit.

With time and practice, our ability to stay with pain gets stronger, and the external irritations seem weaker. It takes a long, long, time. But what else are you going to do? The alternative is to spend a lifetime caught in confusion and irritation. Without practice, over time, it usually gets worse, not better.

With practice, our external irritations weaken, but they don't go away. Any degree of practice is wonderful. I've got a lot of practice still to do, but my life stays in a very different state than it used to. That is worth practicing for.

What do you feel like? Right at this second? The only thing that matters is to experience that. And try to do no harm as you battle through what you're battling through. A lot of factors make this turning possible. What you read makes a difference. Whether you sit every day makes a difference. There are lots of things that assist practice, but we don't really want to do any of them. That's why continuity of practice is so important: to sit when you just think it's pointless. To label your thoughts even if you think this is the dumbest thing you've ever heard of. Each of these things increases your clarity so you can begin to see what you're doing and feeling. If you don't do it, that's fine. You'll suffer for a while. It's okay.

Confidence in What Is

The more you're able to stay with those painful feelings, the more you gain self-confidence in your ability to handle things. Practice is more difficult when you're just struggling to survive. But even when we are in a place where we are not focused on getting our basic needs met, we still struggle, sometimes just as hard. There are all degrees of devastation. With practice, even if the level of devastation gets a little worse, our confidence begins to build. We know we can be okay, at least up to a certain point; we have a lot of confidence. Total confidence would mean we were 100 percent comfortable with life being what it is and us being what we are. I have a lot of confidence, but by no means 100 percent. I could handle just about anything. It doesn't mean I want to, but I know I could. I still notice "I can't" arising, but it comes and goes more quickly.

Each time we sit, we build our ability to stay with who we are, which is always painful. Until we can stay there, it's not yet a strong practice. It may be a practice, but it's not a strong practice until we can stay with ourselves as we really are. Who we really are, this true self, is so different from our ideas about who we are, what somebody else did to me, or what I'd like to do to somebody else. Learning to be with pain is the heart of practice.

PART SIX

RELATIONSHIP

Going into the Dark

THERE IS A famous Sufi teaching story in which a man loses his keys. He is looking for them under the streetlight when his friend walks by. His friend asks, "What are you doing?" The man answers, "I'm looking for my keys." The friend stops to help him look. They search and dig around for a long while. Finally, the friend asks, "Are you sure you lost them here?" And the man replies, "No, I lost them back there somewhere in the dark." His friend stops, astonished, and says, "Well, then why are you looking for them here?" And the man says, "It's so much easier to see."

This is what we do with our life. We have a problem sitting in the dark. We don't really know what to do about it, so we look where it's light. In other words, we look where we're used to looking. Whether it's a problem with relationships, work, or whatever, we tend always to look and to act according to what we're used to. And do you think the man found his keys under the streetlight? No way. Often, we don't even mind if we can't find the keys. What we want is an easy way to look.

There is a darkness out of which everything comes, an endless creative potential that's pouring out of our life at every second. Practice is about going into that darkness. But we're not interested in that. We're interested in looking at life in a way that doesn't disturb us. It may not solve the problem, but, for human beings, that's not really a big issue. Often, we would rather be safe than free.

We want to stay where we're used to. Just think of anything in your life and notice that the only way you handle it is the way you're used to handling it. We tend to look at the surface of things. For instance, hardly a week goes by without somebody saying, "Why do you have so much ritual at the Zen Center?" Having ritual or not having ritual, that's not the problem. That's looking at the surface of things. Some people, since the Zen Center has become relatively big, don't like it as well as when it was small. That is also looking at the surface of things. We look the way we're used to looking.

Because the core belief is a fixed, rigid assemblage of thoughts, it keeps running our lives in a very false way. That's what we do. We don't necessarily like our core belief, but we're used to it. To disrupt it, or anything else we're used to, is frightening. We don't want things to change very much. We don't want our partner to change; we don't want to have to look at ourselves in a way that would wake us up and make us change.

As human beings, we like things to be fixed. We're always trying to control the world so we can be safe. But in doing so, we make the world very small, seemingly more manageable—like a pigeonhole. This disposition is very noticeable in our relationships. When we get into relationships, we tend to do what we've always done. We put them into the same little mold, and we take a look and deliver our opinion, and that's that. Our relationship may become sterile, quarrelsome, polite, or dead, but we stay in our same way of being. It doesn't work.

A Relationship between Teachers

Any relationship, especially a long-term or committed relationship, is a relationship between teachers. And the first thing a teacher needs to do in any relationship is to see what goes on inside themselves. If something is disturbing me in my relationship, my first impulse is to look under the streetlight and say, "Well, there's something wrong with the other person." And we skip the only part of it that matters which is, "What really is going on inside me?"

Looking under the streetlight can look good from the outside. You're being so industrious; you're looking very hard. But it's a pseudo-activity; there's no real movement. We can only tell what's truly going on when we turn back to ourselves.

Say somebody hurts your feelings and you don't want to react. All of us have some habitual way we shut out what that feels like, until everything is kind of numb. "I'll just ignore it. I'm not going to get into it." But there's a big difference between ignoring something and experiencing it. When we ignore something, it's a form of reaction. If I ignore you and whatever you're doing that displeases me, that's still a reaction, and a painful one at that. It may be really polite. Some people stay married fifty years just being polite. That's a graveyard with a lot of bones rattling around under the surface.

Often, we don't look into the painful places because we're afraid of stirring things up. We don't want things to change or end, even if they're not working. Whenever we lose somebody we don't want to lose, there will be grief. But what we often do is turn grief into anguish through blaming them and blaming ourselves. We force ourselves to get very, very busy doing something else. Yet the only real thing would be to feel it. You need to be the grief and embrace it like you would a baby. Just let it be there.

Whenever a relationship has any tension in it—anything unresolved, any dishonesty—there's pain there. That's the only place to look—not at what's wrong with the other person; that doesn't help anything. "They should be different." Or, "It was all my fault. If only I had been blah blah blah."

To experience pain produces transformation. It doesn't necessarily mean the pain goes away, but it's as though it has a big space around it. It's different and you *know* it's different. But we don't want to do that. That's like going into the dark. We don't want to look in the dark of ourselves. And that's why practice is not some formula. Dharma talks are one thing, but the actual practice is the thing that makes our life have depth and richness. You can't just trot out your preformulated understanding. To have relationships work, to be able to experience pain or grief, is a growing maturity within our self. It's a struggle; we don't want to do that. We want to stay under the streetlamp. It isn't about making something that hurts us go away but about the space that opens up. The hurt isn't going to finish you off. Practice concerns the growth of your life such that it's bigger, more spacious. It has more room for you *and* for the person you're in difficulty with. That's real maturing, and, like all maturing, there's no set formula.

People wonder how working on (with?) your relationships in the world relates to the more traditional ways of practice. But what does it mean to be enlightened except to be more and more spacious, holding more and more without criticism, without this criticizing we do? It's an open feeling for something besides yourself.

Authentic Relationships

UNDERSTANDING OUR CLOSE relationships is the key to everything else. All we are is relatedness. We're not separate. I don't exist, except that there's a rug there for me, and it's that moment of contact with the rug that is my existence. Our existence is just moments of contact. In the present moment, all we can do is to make contact. There isn't any past or future.

The moment we make contact creates my life and your life. Ordinarily, we see it as my life bumping up against your life, and not always happily. There is nothing in the universe except relatedness. This is a concrete reality we can practice with from morning to night. And we need to do this, because understanding our relatedness is the key to the kingdom of awakening.

Three Circles

Picture three concentric circles.

The first circle, the one closest around the center, is our core belief.

The second circle, larger than the first, is the choices and identities we've built that arise out of the core belief. It includes all our guises and roles: we're a helper, a hider, a performer, a bumbler, we're a teacher, a student, a friend, a parent, a child, a lover, an athlete. We all have different identities. These identities and the behaviors we enact from them—our basic strategies— are what you see running around in that second circle.

And the third circle, the largest yet, is everything we relate to: other people, events, and the world around us. Our core belief and basic strategies determine our relationships with everyone and everything in our lives. If my core belief is that I can't be loved, perhaps I'll take on the role of teacher, a strategy from the second circle, so I can look for love and admiration from the third circle. I think that's where I'll get love. I know instinctively that there is a hole here, and I have to get love somewhere. It's an absolute must. We do it within the blink of an eye, and we do it all the time.

We can't have real relationships with other people when we place demands on them. If I have a demand on you, I'm not interested in you. I'm more interested in getting something. We may have this demanding relationship with our children, our lovers, our partners, or our parents as we grow older. We try to get something from them to satisfy our core belief.

Now, of course, we're very, very subtle about how we do this. We may say, "I love you. I just want to do everything for you." That obscures the demand. But until we come to terms with the center, the scream—that core belief about ourselves—our relationships with other people will be strongly about demand. I don't mean that's the only thing happening—it varies, of course, at different times—but the demand is always nearby, shaping the relationship. "I want this relationship to give me what I have not found anywhere else."

Or we put clear conditions on the relationship. I've had many students say to me, "You know, I really love my partner. But out of self-respect, I always make it clear that if there's one lapse, one infidelity, that's it. I'm out." What are you experiencing when you say this? There's terror of being unlovable. There's a need for love to fill a certain thing and be a certain way.

· You have an image of yourself that you don't respect, that doesn't match your ideal, so you need another person to help hold up this image of what you want it to be. You have to make sure they stick to what you want, by making it clear. When you insist on a rule like that in a relationship, you are trying to get security and control. But what you really get is loneliness, a lack of intimacy.

Perhaps you have a partner who isn't doing what you want them to do. You two see things differently. And you're resentful and angry. You think the fault is his, of course. Where else would the fault be? The anger hits you at your core. Perhaps the way you handle this is by fighting with your partner, trying to squeeze something out of him that suits you. Now, any of us who have been in that situation know it's not a good way to go about things. We may do it, but we know it doesn't work.

Another thing we do is determine that the other person is against us. We assume that we know what another person is like, so we can confirm that they oppose us. But we don't know them, not really. We can see facets of their behavior, but the biggest error in the world is thinking we ever know what another person is truly like. Even if you've lived with somebody for thirty years, you don't know what they're like.

Very few people know what they're really like, themselves.

Finding a Cover

If your core belief is that you're unlovable, you have to find a world that loves you. You want to fall in love. I used to fall in love with one person after another. If I was wearing one out, I always had another one lined up because I didn't want to be left alone with my core belief, and falling in love covered that up. If there was one man who was fading, I'd be out cultivating another one. I did this for years. I created a lot of mischief, too. I didn't have a practice. I didn't have a clue as to what I was doing. As I did this, I created endless pain for other people and myself.

None of us want to feel that we're absolutely unacceptable to the human race. We can't live that way; it's too painful. And so our basic strategies emerge. We spend most of our time trying to figure out a way to feel anything but this pain.

Where Choice Comes From

The first ring, our core belief, expands into what we think of as our personality: I'm a very shy person; I'm a very retiring person. Out of that core belief comes what I am going to use to push at the outside world in order to get what I want. I want other people to do what I want them to do. "I want you to leave me alone." "I want you to think I'm wonderful." "I want you to give me respect."

We may think we have this under control. But when life begins to hit hard, whether it's an event or something happening with a person, the scream of our own unbearable worthlessness arises: "Why is this happening to me?" We blame other people, accusing them. Mostly, we blame ourselves.

When we operate from this painful core belief of "I can't do it. I'm not good enough. I always fail," we're not free. We see everyone as a potential need-filler. Can you be my teacher? Can you be my partner? Can you be the one who opens up my life for me?

Or, we see everyone as a potential threat. If I've been severely pushed around as a child, really hurt and beaten up and that sort of thing, my strategies are much more apt to be aggressive. "I'll make sure nobody pushes me around anymore. I'll do the pushing, thank you."

Either way, we're being run. We think we're running our lives, but our core beliefs are running the show. We all have major problems in our lives, of one sort or another. But whether we just deal with the problem or let our core belief deal with it is another story. Is my true self in charge, or is it something else? Now, the reason we sit is because we finally understand we must face this. And, if we persevere over time, our true self gets stronger. It feels good, if nothing else. It feels really good. We still have problems, but they're different. We have some awareness of when we can make choices.

Genuine Motivation

As long as our ambition is driven by the core belief, it may be successful in the eyes of the world, but it will never be satisfying. There may come a point where you think you have everything you want, and then either you have a real-life crisis or you implode from the inside. This is because your false self has been driving you ahead, always trying to stay one step ahead of the monkey on your back, which is riding along in great shape because it's getting a free ride on your ambition. Then, at some point, it's likely to fall apart very badly. And even if it doesn't, you may still be living a life of quiet desperation.

Some people have very successful lives, and some people have very satisfying lives. They can look the same, but the thing that's driving those lives is different. Practice is about moving out of a life that's falsely driven into one that has a genuine motivation.

The Other Side of the Mountain

How do you step forward from the
top of a hundred-foot pole?
—*Gateless Gate* case forty-six

PICTURE YOURSELF STANDING on top of this pole. A hundred feet is way up there. Have you ever seen pictures from a thirty-foot diving board? If it were me up there, I'd be terrified. The water looks very far away. If you don't hit it just right, you might die. That pole is not for beginners. If we don't know how to get down from that hundred-foot pole, we're in trouble.

Suppose it's a hazy day up there, and we can't see the ground. We don't know what's down below. Maybe we just woke up on top of this pole and we don't know anything about what's below. It could be three dozen feather beds, which would be just fine. If you're up there, you'd love to know that the pole is surrounded by feather beds. But it could be rocks. It could be deep water, which isn't that bad if you have an idea of how you might get into that water and out again. The rocks would be worse. The feather beds, though, are what interest us most. Feather beds are very soft. The koan itself isn't clear on what's below. It could be anything.

Feather Beds Are Made of Expectations

In life, we try to have feather beds. We pick our friends and even our work, if we can, because we think they will be feather beds. We think we are going to land lightly. We pick a partner because we feel relaxed and happy with that person. They understand our jokes. They think we're great. We think we found a nice soft bed. And this partner perhaps thinks they've got a feather bed in us, too.

This usually goes well for a while, two feather beds together. It's like the early stages of practice. But inevitably there comes a day when there's some suffering. Maybe one of you got laid off and is miserable. The other person tries hard—we all know the rules—to be understanding, supportive, and sympathetic. But then maybe they get ill. Now, you're both suffering, and there's no soft bed to land on.

We enter practice because we think it's a feather bed. "I'm going to be enlightened! It's going to be a different world for me! I'll be at peace! Everything will be wonderful!" Then you begin to sit, and pretty soon it's painful and confusing. Expectation is a life based on the core belief. Expecting your partner will be a certain way. Expecting you'll be a certain way. Expecting that life will be a certain way if you just work hard enough.

Relationships are confusing because we habitually use them to try and make us feel better. We want our partner to be a perfect feather bed, and we have all our requirements for what the partner is supposed to look like, what traits they should and shouldn't have. If we're honest about it, our ideal featherbedder would have to fulfill a long list of requirements. Sometimes we decide to compromise and make do with a marginal featherbedder. But if we have one we're going to adopt as our very own, it should fulfill our list. And the whole thing is a dream. No real relationship is all downy pillows and feathers.

Some people think raising a child is going to be their feather bed. Forget it. It doesn't work that way. Instead of a bunch of people resting in their soft beds, we have a world at war. The pain of not getting what we want is so predominant, it keeps us from being honest, genuine, and connected.

Feather beds are made of your expectations. You decide that your wonderful partner isn't doing anything right. Or they're quiet for a moment, and you decide they think you're the wrong feather bed. They might be doing nothing. When people do nothing, this is particularly insulting.

Now, your bed somehow has lumps. Here we are. We thought we had something perfectly soft, and we don't. We're disappointed. This feather bed is ending up just as lumpy as all the previous feather beds. Often, we get self-righteously angry. The anger is a good cover for the pain underneath.

We may think if we could just understand what's going on, we could fix it. There's nothing wrong with trying to understand your partner. But usually, if we focus on that, we're also removing ourselves from the real emotional base of the whole difficulty. There's no way to "fix" the relationship without turning first to our own expectations and our desire to be distracted from our own pain.

Holding Patterns

A lot of teaching is just "holding." A student is at a particular point in their practice, and you are there with them, using examples and doing things. As the person keeps experiencing and learning and struggling, maybe they begin to see more clearly here and there. But teaching is a holding pattern for a long time. And then something happens. Maybe it's the accumulation of practice. Maybe life keeps throwing different things into the pot. Suddenly a strong shift appears.

Any good, close relationship can be in this holding pattern. It's not giving way to this or that, believing this or believing that, or acting too soon. It's just holding and letting the practice, the relationship, slowly create what it always creates if we practice with our most honest effort. Our ability to do this with everything we have increases over time.

The first insights are always in the mind. And then that psychological layer starts lengthening and deepening itself. You can't always see that on the surface; all you see are the surface troubles we're immersed in. But that slowly growing depth is the holding. A good teacher understands what it means to hold. You don't expect people to change in two weeks. A holding pattern can take years sometimes.

You have to have patience with that holding. We don't get a formula or a timeline. What keeps us in the holding, even if we don't know when it will shift, is aspiration. It's that possibility of the other side of the mountain that is in each one of us. If we can feel that, it will drive our practice and our relationships. Who you are is life itself. The knowing and understanding that comes out of that recognition can hold a lot.

Things as They Are

Imagine you are living on one side of a huge mountain. On the other side of that mountain is something more wonderful than anything you've ever seen before. You could live there, but since you've never seen it, you don't even know how to picture it. You consider it for a minute, and then you go back to trying to live in the mess you've always lived in.

Being in real relationship, with a beloved or with life in general, can lead us to the other side of that mountain—not all the time, not consistently—but more and more. It's difficult to describe, though it's not theoretical. Until you've felt genuine relationship, it's difficult to imagine. Most of us can't exert ourselves for something that we can't see. We exert ourselves to keep fixing what seems fixable. It's usually only when we find we can't fix the things outside of us that practice gets serious. The very nature of our practice is to see through the expectations and illusions in our relationships.

The only way to see the other side of the mountain is to be with everything. There really isn't another side of the mountain and this side of the mountain. There's just this moment, and being with whatever it is—your own anger, your partner's anger, or whatever it might be. If we can truly do that and not get lost in our ideas about it, then we begin to see the other side of the mountain.

A lot of practice is just patience. You may not quite see what has to be done next, but you have to have the patience to just sit down and do your practice. It may not seem as though much is happening. But the brain is beginning to release all sorts of things. Things are surfacing. Without patience, life is never going to feel like the other side of the mountain. Even though every moment is the other side of the mountain. There couldn't be anything else. There is always only one thing to do: be with things as they are. Those can seem like simple words, but it's practice, a lot of practice, that enables us to do this.

A Dagger Passing Through

A TEACHER'S JOB is to absorb, when necessary, the student's dagger. If those daggers bother you quite a bit, you certainly shouldn't be teaching. Even if they bother you more than once in a while, you shouldn't be teaching. Because if it bothers you, if the dagger causes you pain, you can't see clearly. You are blinded, and the teacher's job is to see a student clearly.

When it comes to our close relationships, it doesn't take much of a dagger to arouse that blindness. And the closer the relationship, the more easily the dagger goes in, the more we feel it, and the harder it is to heal. Often, the greatest wounds come from our families of origin. In many ways, we are our parents—there is no way to not be our parents, because we come from them. The anger and pain from that relationship is often our greatest wound.

But, as a teacher, we can learn to hold space so the dagger passes right through. We don't grow up overnight. Yamada Roshi said that Zen practice is about the development of character. I think that means the ability to hold to your practice when someone is attacking you. You have some idea of what their welfare might be, even as they're going after you. Any teacher who's genuinely trying to do a good job teaching gets attacks all the time. To hold to the welfare of another person when your own welfare is being assaulted, that's tough. Sometimes, I have a tough time and I'll think, "It's time to retire; I'm sick of this." And I continue to practice. Then, like all of us, I start to experience this reactivity, and something amazing happens. There's a moment of sudden comprehension where I see life in a different way and continue to teach.

Teachers, Not Saviors

The aim isn't to cling to the teacher but to be free of the teacher. Yet until we're truly free within ourselves, our strategies and habits are so strong that we all need somebody to remind us a little bit of the path.

Of course, your teacher messes up as often as anybody else. Sometimes, they don't have any idea what practice is about. This is only a problem if we think they should help fix us. The human dream is to want something or someone to save us, and we have our Zen style for this: a perfect teacher, a perfect practice. I'm not going to save you; I don't even want to. I've got enough things I can do besides that. It's not personal. I'm not trying to save anybody.

If there's anything to learn here, you have to learn it by yourself. I can give you some guidance. But, believe me, I can't do it for you. And I'm not interested in doing it for you. I don't care if you're miserable, okay? Who cares? What I'm interested in is the only thing that practice can do anything about, which is helping you get clear and understand your basic core belief. It's this basic thing that I'm most interested in.

Deep Listening

Are you listening? That's the most important question a teacher, or any of us, can ask ourselves. When I started to teach, I hadn't really learned to listen. I would listen, and then the next thing I noticed, my mind was off somewhere else. After a lot of training and practice, my mind now stays out of the way more so I can listen. I am more and more aware that my thinking isn't real, and I'm much more interested in staying with what is real. Listening is the greatest gift I can give you as a teacher, and the greatest gift you can give another person.

When you feel deep listening from another person, you're encouraged. You have hope. You begin to feel, "Oh, maybe I can do this too." Your life becomes more enjoyable and appreciative. The lives that you touch tend to feel those qualities, and they become more enjoyable and appreciative as well.

PART SEVEN

WONDER

Far from Shore

One does not discover new lands without consenting
to lose sight, for a very long time, of the shore.
—*André Gide*, The Counterfeiters

GOING TO NEW lands sounds wonderful. But the last thing we want is to lose sight of the shore. The shore is life as we've come to know it—the troubling and painful yet familiar life of our core belief. To practice is to lose sight of the shore and spend a lot of time at sea. Initially, we consent to leaving our shore because we want to get to these new lands we've heard about. We no longer quite believe in the shore we've always lived on, but we're not able to see the new shore either. We're just at sea, and we feel disturbed because we're unanchored, so we focus on thinking about how we're on our way to somewhere wonderful.

Over time, we realize that we don't know where we're going—we're just lost at sea. We feel seasick. We're sick of practice and sick of feeling so much. We can't go back to the old shore again; we know too much to do that. But we don't know where we're going.

Drifting at Sea

When we're in this in-between place, which is really where we spend the majority of our practice, we're working with fear. It's hard not to have certainty. We don't have the life that, whether we liked it or not, was familiar with misery. And we don't have the new land—or, more accurately, we think we don't.

We feel discouraged, bored, and disillusioned. At times we feel totally confused and angry. At times we have a powerful urge to go back to where it's safe. But we also have a tremendous longing for a life lived more truly, which we've glimpsed through the fog. Maybe there's a thin sliver of something on the horizon, but maybe not. You're just in the middle of nowhere. What happens if you're willing to be in this sea, in this sense of helplessness?

Spiritual traditions tend to emphasize seeing the new land. But most of our practice and time is spent drifting in the struggle. Perhaps, just possibly, what we finally get to see is that being on the shore, struggling in the open ocean, and being in the new land are all the same. There's nowhere to go. Or, put differently: this shore is it; out on the desolate ocean is it; the other shore is it. There's simply being at peace with wherever you are.

So, why launch off from the shore in the first place? What is the point if it seems to be untold uncertainty and struggle, with no new land to arrive at? Our practice is not to arrive somewhere, but to see that these three "places" are the same, and that we have already arrived.

To do this, we need to just be the struggle. There is nothing except being what you are. At some point, we just roll over on our back and float, and nothing's different, and everything is different.

Ninety-Nine Tries

There was a man who struggled for years. Though he spent twenty years practicing with a renowned teacher, he never quite seemed to deepen his understanding. The teacher just pushed him and pushed him: "Try this . . . Okay, try this . . . Hmmm, try this." Then one day, the man got it. Becoming quite mad, he went to his teacher and said, "I can't believe I did all that struggling for twenty years only to realize that you don't need the struggle." And the teacher said, "If I had spared you your struggle, you would have never seen that there's no struggle necessary."

You have to work at your practice. Try this and try that and try that. You have to be alert. Watch yourself trying if you want. When the day comes that you see that that's all nonsense, fine. But take heed of what the master said.

Yasutani Roshi used to say that the fact that you hit the bull's-eye on the hundredth attempt doesn't mean that it had nothing to do with the ninety-nine tries. It has a lot to do with the ninety-nine tries. As you engage in that struggle, no matter how you do it, if there's any awareness, then you're maturing. You're changing into what you always were.

Do Good

THE BASIC VOW of practice is to do good. Don't harm, just do good. This doesn't mean to *try* and do good, because that trying is thinking. It means to *do* good. You can't do good if you're mad at somebody and want to do them in. That's impossible. You can't do good if you're spending most of your time trying to defend yourself from the world. That's also impossible.

We get good at what we practice. So, what do we want to get good at? Look at what kind of life you want to live and whether your actions are going in that direction. With practice, we can differentiate the strategy of doing good that is dictated by our core belief from the good that flows out of us living our true life. We clarify the difference between a self-centered and a life-centered effort.

As you sit, you may gain an understanding, very slowly over time and without trying to do anything about it, that the purpose of your life is just to be yourself. That doesn't mean to be yourself in the ordinary sense. It means to be your true self, a self that does good. Only then does what we call a life of service begin to open up. I don't mean that you're all of a sudden running around serving people. Though it could look like that. But more deeply, the whole feeling of your life changes, and what you care most about is doing no harm to others and repairing any harm that has been done.

I'm not saying go out and save the world. But people who practice regularly do change the world. A good practice changes anyone who comes into contact with it. However, if you think you're going to run around and change people, you'll notice they begin to avoid you. I'll avoid you too.

Sacrifice

In Zen practice, we spend a lot of time sitting. If we hurt, we sit. If we don't hurt, we sit. We sit long hours. Do you think of those hours of sitting as sacrifice? A student said to me, "Well, I know you've been very ill, and I know you're just sacrificing your life for your students." That surprised me. I don't think of practice as sacrifice. I don't think of teaching or sitting as sacrifice. I think what I'm doing is fun. Because sitting is the same thing as living. In practicing and in living with more awareness, all we are sacrificing is our illusions.

Say you get up early to sit in meditation when you really don't want to. The bed is warm, and you just really would like to stay in it and sleep some more. But you get up because sitting helps make your life whole. The practice begins the very second you get up. Because, in that moment, you have enough awareness to see that the sitting, in the long run, is what you want to do. You aren't losing something by sitting; you are finding your wholeness.

In Buddhism, there is the concept of the Bodhisattva vow—a commitment to liberate all sentient beings. That's the idea. The reality might be that we'd rather go to the corner and get a hot fudge sundae. If our reality is that we'd rather be elsewhere, then we will likely feel annoyed that we have to give up something in order to be there for someone else.

The Bodhisattva vow can be an idealized goal, a head on top of our own head—another excuse to keep us from experiencing our life as it is. A genuine part of us is drawn toward easing suffering. This is great, as long as we don't get caught in the idea of "sacrificing ourselves." Sometimes it isn't appropriate to take on someone else's suffering. We'd be better off letting them go through their own pain and learn their own strength.

If we define our lives as giving up something, we're always sacrificing. When we live our lives with compassion and awareness, we realize we're actually gaining a lot in any situation. We express and act from compassion for its own sake. And, in turn, our life becomes rich and full.

Serve Yourself

It's easy to save the world in your head. It's no trouble at all to have noble thoughts about this or that way of saving things. Until we embody this desire and have the felt experience of living it in our daily lives, it's just another strategy, another escape.

You may say you vow to save all sentient beings. How many are there? There are millions of them. If you're trying to save all sentient beings, you're trying to fix something, usually in your-self. The only way you can save all sentient beings is to be your true self. When you are your true self at least a fair amount of the time—because no one I've yet met is there 100 percent of the time—you begin to be a beneficial presence in the world.

To be of service is a koan in and of itself. What does it mean to serve yourself, to serve someone else, and to serve a situation? It doesn't mean to be running around straightening everything out and trying to help everyone. Some people wear themselves out serving others. When your health is threatened, when your equilibrium is threatened, it is difficult to truly serve. Serving others includes taking care of yourself.

To be of service sometimes means to be very helpful to someone else. Sometimes it means to give up almost everything you have. And sometimes it means to keep everything you have. A good practice leads to service and to doing the work. That can look very different on different people, but one way you know you're doing this work is that it feels spacious. In a practice sense, if you are not being yourself, you're not being of service.

Now, some of you think it's enough to say, "I really don't want to serve anybody." That may be honest, but it doesn't have any integrity in it. Service and willingness to do the work flows nat-urally out of a good practice. This doesn't mean we work all the time. It means there is less separation between being of service, doing the work, and living our true lives.

Narrow Is the Way

For the gate is narrow and the way is hard that
leads to life, and those who find it are few.

—Matthew 7:14*

THE OTHER DAY, I was trying to find a tennis match on
television and instead bumped into a boxing match. As far as I
can tell, the point of boxing is to injure the other person's brain,
which isn't exactly the greatest thing to do. But still, I found
myself drawn to watching. This match was between two extremely skilled boxers. I don't understand boxing particularly,
but it was obvious that these guys were good at what they were
doing. I watched for a while, fascinated by each punch. There was
an immediacy to the contact.

We spend the majority of our lives not connecting, and we
sense there is a connection missing. Maybe that's why I found
myself fascinated by the boxing match: it demands everything of
its participants in a small ring and a very short period of time. I
was struck by the immediacy—such an immediate experience of

---

* Revised English Version.

pain. This is true for other sports, such as football, as well. Perhaps that's why people like to watch them, to experience that connection. Think of a matador, who has to stand there with full attention with that big bull charging around. The bull is amazing, but it's the matador we're fascinated by, that he can be so fully present, holding ground.

The Easy Way

Students often complain to me, "I've been practicing for a while now, labeling my thoughts, and once in a while, I do something I think is experiencing. But actually, I don't feel any better. So, what's the point of all this hard work?" This is quite an understandable question.

We all want results. We think that practice will give us the connection that's missing in our lives. We do it because we think it's supposed to give us wonderful things.

Say you wanted to become a great pianist, like Arthur Rubinstein. You have this ambition, so for a year, you read all the books on how to play and on the lives of the great masters. You learn the history of music. You listen to great pianists play. You study hard. But you don't go near the piano. And then, after a year, you wonder why you aren't a brilliant pianist.

It's amazing how we approach Zen practice the same way. We all want to be Arthur Rubinstein. We don't want to be the person who can bang out a little tune. But even just to bang out a little tune is not easy. The desire for that big thing overrides our doing the hard work. The easy way is to dream, to think, to look at the pictures, and to read the books.

Playing a sport or an instrument extremely well is not just thoughts, ideas, and theories. It's embodied. And until our true self is embodied almost constantly, we will not have our true life, the one we really want.

There are ways that we're all boxing, though it doesn't usually look like opening up somebody's face with a good uppercut. We're in the boxing ring of life with our partners, our jobs, our circumstances. Most of the time, we're actually not in the ring—we've wandered over by the wall and are shadowboxing. In boxing, you're trying to jab the other person in the head. Shadowboxing is just jabbing a shadow, with no real contact. And most of our thinking is shadowboxing. Part of waking up to the present moment is to become aware of the fact that, usually, we're just shadowboxing and not making contact with life.

We don't want to think that everything we do all day long is the way, and therefore deserves our true attention, our true contact. We want the easy way. This is just the nature of being human. If I were to take every problem that people bring me, hundreds of questions and problems every week, they all boil down to the same problem: "I want the easy way."

It doesn't help to say we're going to take the hard way. That's useless. We still don't take the hard way; we take the easy way. The way to begin is to see through what the easy way is. Which of our behaviors, belief systems, and actions are the easy way?

We rarely know the answer here, because the heart of the easy way is not to pay attention. We all have our pseudo-ways of paying attention. We do this by trying to fix people outside ourselves. We project everything onto the outside world, so that in some way somebody else is responsible for this mess. Perhaps we start practicing, with the hope that we'll become less irritable or more immune to difficulties.

Glittering Images

The gate is narrow, but on the other side is the immediacy and juiciness of true life.

We all have glittering images of the way we are, the way we think we should be, the way other people should be, and the way our life should be. Our true self is always blocked by our glittering images.

It's very common with people who do any kind of practice to have a glittering image of themselves. It's fine to do a lot of things and to do them well, but it's very easy to make them into part of our glittering image of ourselves. We have to pay attention that we don't turn our skill into the easy way. You have to do the work of inspecting who it is that thinks they're performing the skill. Whose mass of frozen emotions are these? Who is the doer?

When we undertake an activity without attention, whether it's sitting practice, sports, piano, or anything, then it becomes the easy way. If you get good at something, you can add it to your glittering image collection. Perhaps you think, "Well I'm not so bad after all. I can do this." The core belief is as strong as ever.

Sitting can very well become the easy way. Zen practice and sitting can be the biggest escape there is if you stop paying attention. You have to reach some maturity in yourself so you can be aware if this happens. A teacher can help.

A particular human ideal is to have the easy way but to dress it up as being very difficult. When we dress up our strategies that way, they become particularly lethal, because other people tend to look up to us. They think we really know something, and that reinforces our own belief that we do too.

Ordinary Wonder

A lot of people who practice begin to feel a little freedom. This is probably the best way to describe a life that is less and less caught by self-centered attachments. It's free. It's also flexible. It's kind. And it's fun. We forget about fun. A life without fun is miserable. You know instinctively when you meet a person who has a little bit of freedom. There's just something different about them.

As your core belief fades, fixed thoughts, ideals, and glittering images are no longer running your life. And when they fade, things go better. Life gets a little clearer, a little more spacious. I don't mean you're always happy. But there's a fundamental rightness to your life that begins to appear.

Practice is the slow effacement—usually over many, many years—of this false master called the core belief. You efface the fixed picture of how you should be. And when you efface it, you don't replace it with another fixed picture called "enlightenment."

Through practice, we begin to see through the rigid views we've had of the world. It's not like we suddenly wake up from a dream, though there are moments of that. But usually, it's just faint effacement going on all the time. And as we wear away the picture, life becomes more real, more fluid. We're in life, flowing along with it. It's almost impossible to put into words.

We're tempted to focus on what we imagine enlightenment is rather than to experience living with a little more fluidity and freedom. It's the image of enlightenment that's the problem. True enlightenment, since it can't even be talked about, is not a thing. We don't need to worry about it.

You can't imagine the freedom to be your true self. It's an absence, and you can't pick up an absence. You can only slowly just get to be that way. The longer we practice, the more we have a clue about how to slowly become free. Freedom is the name of the game. Freedom to be nothing. It doesn't mean that you vanish or that you don't enjoy a good meal. It's not some spooky thing. It's an ordinary wonder.

AFTERWORD
by Brenda Beck Hess

FOR MANY OF us, our lives are filled with challenges and hardships: we suffer. Charlotte Joko Beck's life was also just like this, albeit with her particular circumstances. Suffering drove her on a relentless quest to make sense of the pain and cruelty she found in her life, and to find peace. Finally, this search took her to Zen practice.

As brought to Westerners from Japan, Zen practice could seem quite austere and inaccessible. With its Japanese terminology, concepts like *satori* or enlightenment often seemed incomprehensible. The esoteric and existential puzzles from the lives of ancient Zen figures felt remote, more like an exotic lifestyle or mystical adornment than an embodied, immediate practice.

Joko's gift was to speak about practice with her students in a way that stripped away many of the trappings of the religion. Her teachings were practical and precise, applicable to each of us in our daily lives. She felt the ordinary stuff of our lives—relationships, work, financial problems—were the wonderful fodder for our practice. She never wavered, though, from the importance of daily meditation practice as the way to develop our strength of practice, to have a quiet space with which to reveal the habitual patterns and beliefs that run our lives. Ultimately, sitting quietly allows us the space to experience the pain usually hidden within all this.

Ordinary Wonder is one of the products of this teaching, clearly outlining the path we must walk with commitment and persistence. What is most clear from Joko's writings is that this path is extraordinarily simple. This does not mean it is easy to walk this path; indeed, it requires everything we have. However, by actually doing this practice, Joko shows that each of us has the ability to increase the freedom and peace in our lives—to learn, ultimately, what this no-thing called enlightenment is.